OCS Study
MMS 2002-011

# Socioeconomic and Environmental Issues Analysis of Oil and Gas Activity on the Outer Continental Shelf of the Western Gulf of Mexico

I0439165

## Final Report

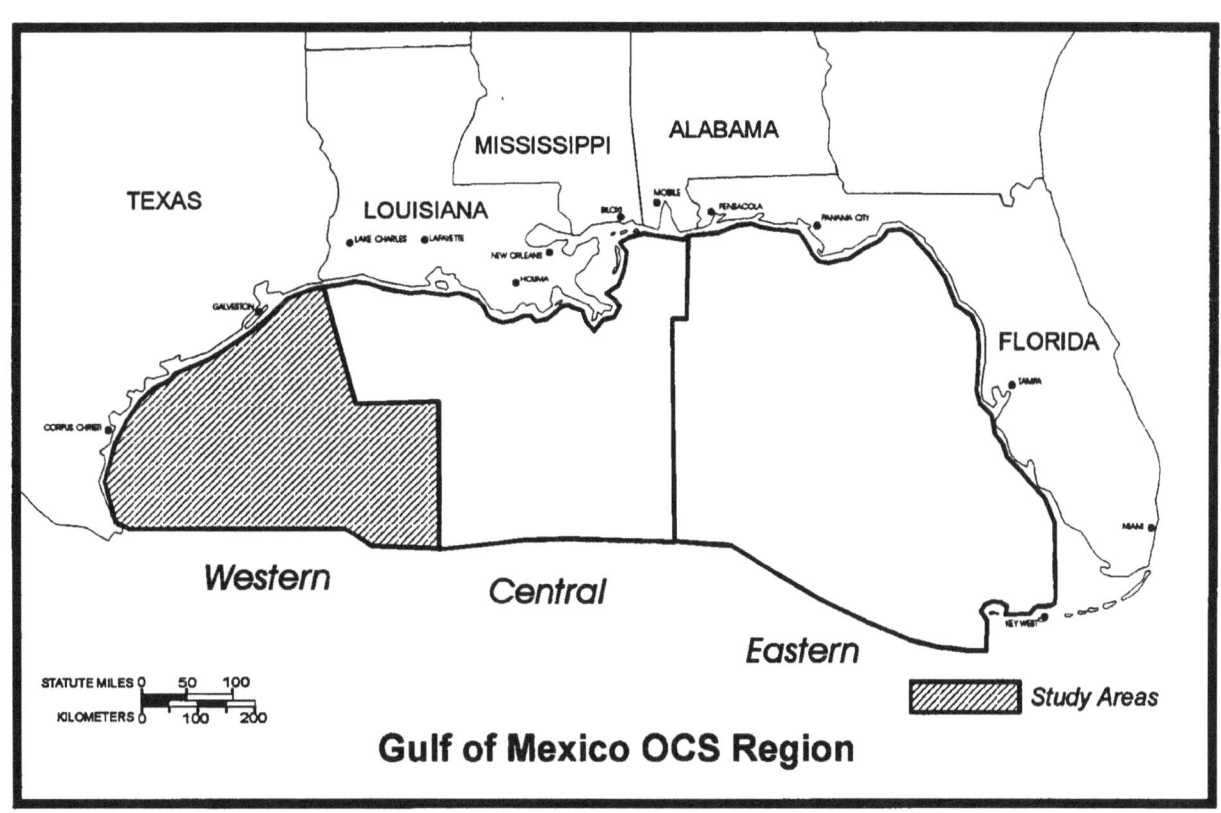

Gulf of Mexico OCS Region

**U.S. Department of the Interior**
**Minerals Management Service**
**Gulf of Mexico OCS Region**

OCS Study
MMS 2002-011

# Socioeconomic and Environmental Issues Analysis of Oil and Gas Activity on the Outer Continental Shelf of the Western Gulf of Mexico

## Final Report

Author

William R. Kelley

Prepared under MMS Contract
14-35-0001-30797
by
Louisiana State University
Baton Rouge, Louisiana  70803

Published by

**U.S. Department of the Interior**
**Minerals Management Service**
**Gulf of Mexico OCS Region**

**New Orleans**
**March 1999**

# DISCLAIMER

This report was prepared under contract between the Minerals Management Service (MMS) and Louisiana State University. This report has been technically reviewed by the MMS and approved for publication. Approval does not signify that the contents necessarily reflect the views and policies of the Service, nor does mention of trade names or commercial products constitute endorsement or recommendation for use. It is, however, exempt from review and compliance with MMS editorial standards.

# REPORT AVAILABILITY

Extra copies of the report may be obtained from the Public Information Office (Mail Stop 5043) at the following address:

> U.S. Department of the Interior
> Minerals Management Service
> Gulf of Mexico OCS Region
> Public Information Office (MS 5034)
> 1201 Elmwood Park Boulevard
> New Orleans, Louisiana 70123-2394
> Telephone Numbers: 1-800-200-GULF or (504) 736-2519

# CITATION

Suggested citation:

Kelley, W.R. 2002. Socioeconomic and Environmental Issues Analysis of Oil and Gas Activity on the Outer Continental Shelf of the Western Gulf of Mexico; Final Report. OCS Study MMS 2002-011. U.S. Dept. of the Interior, Minerals Mgmt. Service, Gulf of Mexico OCS Region, New Orleans, La. 72 pp.

# TABLE OF CONTENTS

# A SOCIOECONOMIC AND ENVIRONMENTAL ISSUES ANALYSIS OF OIL AND GAS ACTIVITY IN THE OUTER CONTINENTAL SHELF OF THE WESTERN GULF OF MEXICO

## 1. Introduction

This study focuses on the social, economic, and environmental issues related to the oil and gas industry which are salient to members of communities in five selected counties located on or near the coast of the Gulf of Mexico in southeast Texas. The primary goal of this project is to identify the issues and concerns of stakeholder groups in the coastal region, as well as to understand the relationships among various issues and groups. Ultimately, this information should facilitate communication between these stakeholder groups and those who make policy decisions that affect their communities.

## 2. Background Information and Recent Developments

The Texas coastal region has been heavily invested in the oil and gas industry since 1901, when a well in the Spindletop oil field in Jefferson County "blew" in a gusher. This discovery of mass quantities of oil in southeast Texas quickly resulted in Texas becoming the center of the nation's oil industry. It also was the catalyst for unprecedented industrial development in the state as the region became a major refining area. The oil industry flourished through World War II and experienced a major "boom" in the early 1970s, as a result of increased demand, price deregulation, and the oil embargo by Arab countries. As oil prices continued to rise throughout the 70s, money continued to pour into south Texas and many communities along the coast became increasingly dependent on the industry. As the supply and price of oil increased, demand for petroleum products decreased, ultimately resulting in an oil glut and the beginning of a "bust" cycle in the early 1980s. In a very short time, the price of a barrel of oil plunged to $11, down from a previous high of around $40. By the mid-80s, the decline of the industry had caused a major recession in south Texas, causing widespread unemployment, and the collapse of social and economic infrastructures throughout the region.

By the time this study was initiated, recovery was well underway in most of the coastal communities that had been hardest hit by the mid-1980s bust. In some places, recovery has been achieved through efforts to diversify economically (e.g., Houston and Corpus Christi), while other communities have mostly abandoned their prior direct investment in the oil and gas industry and have turned to other sources of economic development, such as tourism (e.g., Rockport, Port Aransas, and Galveston). Still other communities have diversified to a limited extent, but remain heavily dependent on the industry, and are primarily "riding out the hard times," waiting for the fortunes of the industry to turn (Texas City, Beaumont, and Port Arthur).

All of these communities, however, are, to varying degrees, experiencing some economic improvement in the latter half of the 1990s, as compared to the mid- and late-80s. This helps to explain the general optimism evident in discussions with many of the informants. In general, communities on the Texas coast have been intertwined so deeply and for so long with the oil and gas industry that there is little question of its continued presence and socioeconomic influence. One frequently expressed attitude is that while the industry will probably never produce the fortunes that it did in the 1970s and early 80s, it is here to stay and so the best approach is to "get what you can, when you can" from it. While oil and gas reserves in Texas are in no way depleted, the state is now a net importer of oil. The refining sector has become increasingly more dependent upon foreign oil, in part because several major oil companies have moved their operations overseas in response to the increasing globalization of the industry.

Recent technological developments in the area of offshore drilling techniques, however, have created a potential for increased extraction activity in the Gulf of Mexico. Three major discoveries have made the Outer Continental Shelf (OCS) once again an attractive site for investment of oil companies' domestic exploration budgets. First, geologists using 3-D seismic technology have discovered that many mature oil fields on the OCS contain smaller reservoirs that had been previously overlooked. This allows for increased production at established sites. Second, in 1993 Phillips Petroleum became the first company to successfully exploit a sub-salt oil field. Although drilling through layers of salt is expensive and technically difficult at times, the reserves that can be exploited in this way are potentially very productive and profitable; Phillips has announced that they expect to get 100 million barrels from their first sub-salt field. The third development fueling offshore extraction activities is the ability of companies to drill in increasingly deeper waters. In 1994, Shell Oil Company began successfully pumping oil from an offshore platform in the Gulf of Mexico in 2,860 feet of water, 137 miles from shore. In the past, drilling platforms on the OCS have typically been anchored on fixed legs in relatively shallow waters, but the production of huge floating platforms (anchored with mooring cables) and the use of more sophisticated exploration techniques has made deep-water drilling possible for the first time.

In general, the minor "boom" that may result from these developments is very different from the oil boom of the late 70s and early 80s. The oil companies involved are much more cautious and, in many cases, have funded their research by downsizing general operations and reducing their overall number of employees. Oil company supply companies and support industries are more likely to provide jobs and additional money to local communities, but the scope of this development is in no way comparable to the economic contribution of the industry to the area two decades ago. Still, these recent small surges in activity may have affected the data collected for this report. A few of the communities represented in this study have begun to experience some positive results of this increased drilling activity, while others are cautiously optimistic in response to it. No one we talked to thought that the level of oil and gas activity would ever equal that of the 1970s and 80s, but most respondents were pleased with the prospect of any renewed activity in the region.

Oil-related activities in the Gulf of Mexico have had the greatest impact on the state economies and social infrastructures of communities in Louisiana and Texas. While both states have felt the results of the volatility of the oil and gas industry in recent decades, there are some significant differences in regional experience that should be noted. In general, Louisiana has historically been most heavily invested in offshore drilling and in providing support services for these activities. In contrast, Texas has had a more extensive involvement in onshore activities such as the refining and processing of crude oil. Texas has also attracted the corporate offices and benefited from the associated upper-management jobs of several large oil companies (especially in Houston), while most of the oil-related employment opportunities in Louisiana have been in lower level positions. While there are hundreds of gas and oil wells off the Texas coast, the state is still far less dependent on local drilling activity than is Louisiana. In fact, some Texas refineries deal almost exclusively with imported raw materials. This magnifies the importance of ports along the Texas coast, and creates a different situation for Texas coastal communities trying to respond to the fluctuations of the industry as a whole. In general, while both Texas and Louisiana have felt the pains of the 1980s oil bust, involvement in both upstream and downstream activities may have given Texas a slight edge in dealing with its consequences.

The strong presence of the oil and gas industry on the Texas coast (and the dependency of local communities upon its ongoing success) was never disputed by the respondents in this study. Not even the most radical environmental activists that we talked to suggested that the oil industry should "go away" – the direct and indirect dependency of the region on the industry is simply a fact of life. What the communities that live within the context of this dependency want is the freedom to benefit economically from this situation, and at the same time, some assurance that the environment is being protected as much as possible.

### 3. Methodology

The subject matter and primary questions to be considered in this study led to the adoption of a qualitative approach. Our general focus was on the subjective perceptions of individual informants about a number of issues and their perspectives about various aspects of the relationship between the oil and gas industry and Texas coastal communities. An open-ended discussion format allowed for elaboration on issues that were salient to individuals in different areas and with a variety of ties to the industry. It also facilitated the introduction and discussion of unanticipated areas of importance to the respondents. This approach is not appropriate for generalizing to the larger population, so random sampling techniques were not used. Instead, the focus was on ensuring variation in the characteristics of specific informants. This was accomplished by selecting respondents from different sectors of the community and from different geographical locations throughout the coastal region.

### 3.1. Sampling

The primary unit of analysis used in this study was the Texas coastal region. This broad area was divided into existing counties, which provided the primary sampling units. Demographic profiles of all of the counties in the region were assembled, based on data from various federal, state, and local sources. After reviewing the information gathered at this early stage, five counties were pro-actively chosen for inclusion in this study, based on their specific experience and varied levels of involvement with the oil and gas industry. These were Aransas, Galveston, Harris, Jefferson, and Nueces counties.

Regional criteria were used to ensure variation and representative opinions among the informants. For instance, some counties were chosen for inclusion because of their focus on coastal tourism and recreation, others for their investment in downstream industry activities such as refining and petrochemical manufacturing, and still others for their involvement in both downstream and exploration and drilling activities. There was also a mix in terms of the size of the communities located within these county boundaries. Major urban areas (e.g., Houston and Corpus Christi) were targeted, as well as smaller cities and towns (e.g., Beaumont, Port Arthur, Galveston, Texas City, Rockport, and Port Aransas). Aransas County is largely rural, with most of its population located in the Rockport/Fulton area. The population of potential informants was made up of individuals residing in each of these counties.

To ensure a variety of opinions and experiences among participants, we originally targeted community leaders in three primary sectors: business, government (state, county and city levels), and environmental organizations. Because of the inherent limitations of utilizing discussion data, we focused on local leaders in each of the five counties, rather than on the general population. It was assumed that community leaders would be the most knowledgeable about local issues related to the oil and gas industry, and that they could provide us with information about the general attitudes of the residents in their area. The business, government, and environmental sectors provided convenient categories for use in grouping respondents, but they were not mutually exclusive. In many cases, informants represented the opinions of individuals in more than one of the three primary sectors. For example, a city council member also owned a local business, a businessperson was also elected to the local school board, or a representative from an environmental organization worked for the oil and gas industry. Indeed, one finding of this study is that it is erroneous to assume that varying interest groups in this region exist independently of one another. For analytical purposes, in cases where individual respondents could be characterized as representing more than one sector, they were identified as being in the category which best described either their primary involvement or the official position they filled which led to our initial contact with them.

After establishing the three sectors upon which to focus, we began to look for specific individuals to contact within each of these groups. To assist in this effort, we contacted several people whom we assumed were knowledgeable about the issues in each of the targeted areas and requested background information as well as referrals of people to contact for more lengthy interviews. At this stage, we made efforts to contact Texas state senators whose districts were located in the targeted geographical regions and individuals from local newspaper staff in each community. Telephone interviews were conducted with two state senators and media representatives from seven different communities.

These initial interviews provided us with enough information to begin the process of contacting primary informants for face-to-face interviews. Because this approach was so effective, we utilized a snowball sampling technique for the remainder of the data collection process. Referrals from previous interviews were augmented with the names of some specific targeted contacts in each community (e.g., members of local Chambers of Commerce, city council members, county commissioners, and members of specific environmental organizations, such as local chapters of the Sierra Club, the Audubon Society, and other environmental groups).

One observation during this stage of the sampling process that altered our perspective about potential respondents should be noted. Contrary to our expectations, there were no clearly organized, definable "stakeholder groups" in the targeted communities. The influence of the industry in this area is so pervasive that the entire community is strongly affected by industry developments. So many people have direct dealings with the industry through their employment, their physical location in the community, or their business and social interests that to separate out specific "stakeholders" seemed too limiting. We therefore broadened our definition of the pool of prospective informants to include additional categories of people within the targeted communities.

We did not target oil and gas industry representatives at this point, because we planned to include them in focus group discussions to be conducted at a later point in the data gathering stage. The initial interviewing strategy was to conduct approximately 15 face-to-face discussions with individual informants, and then to proceed to a second phase, which included recruiting various individuals with different interests (including the perspective of the industry) to participate in focus groups. We abandoned this strategy for two primary reasons after conducting several face-to-face interviews. First, the interviews were very productive, providing us with very useful and candid information in all of our targeted topical areas. Informants continued to provide additional referrals, and it seemed reasonable to continue gathering information from these individual sources. Second, the people that we were interviewing frequently had direct ties to oil and gas, and were therefore providing us with information from the perspective of the industry. For instance, several of the government officials we interviewed were retired from the industry, and informants from other sectors were currently employed by oil and gas companies. We therefore made the decision to increase the number of face-to-face discussions conducted instead of moving on to gather focus group data. (Refer to Appendix A for a chart containing information about all respondents' county locations and sectors).

## 3.2. Discussions

Dr. Nancy Bell, a member of the research staff for the project, conducted all the discussions. A first round of telephone discussions were completed and a list of targeted referrals established. Afterward, a local research service organization – Tammadge Market Research, Inc. – was hired to make initial contact with potential respondents and schedule meetings if they were interested in participating in the study (the vast majority of people contacted were willing to provide us with the information requested). Dr. Bell coordinated with staff members from Tammadge, and made several trips to the Texas coastal region to conduct the discussions from March through May of 1997.

A total of 39 semi-structured discussions were conducted over this time period. All informants were assured of anonymity, and advised that the information they provided would remain confidential. To ensure some uniformity of topics covered, a discussion guide with specific questions was created (refer to Appendix B for a list of questions used). The general approach was to begin with broad questions, which focused on a particular topic, and then to probe for further information in these areas by using verbal prompts. This strategy worked well, since it allowed informants to elaborate in areas where they had special expertise or interest, and at the same time, kept the interview process somewhat structured. These interviews ranged from 25 minutes to 2 hours in length, with most lasting approximately 45 minutes to an hour.

Since we were utilizing a snowball sampling strategy, we did not establish a specific number of discussions to be conducted. New referrals were scheduled for meetings throughout the process, and data gathering continued until it became clear that we had a sufficient amount of information to continue on the next phase of the project. Our judgment that enough data had been gathered was based on two factors. First, and most important, we had a convergence of information – the majority of perspectives and information being provided by respondents had already been obtained in previous discussions. Second, these meetings were producing fewer new referrals. Many of the individuals that respondents suggested we contact had already been mentioned in prior interview encounters and most had been contacted. All of the face-to-face discussions were audio taped and these tapes were duplicated for security purposes. They were then transcribed by a professional transcribing service and delivered in both hard copy and diskette formats.

In the analysis stage, a content analysis of the recordings was conducted to identify emerging themes. The data were organized around specific topical areas, and comparisons of the perspectives of respondents from different counties, cities, and sectors were made. Verbatim quotes were then lifted from the individual transcripts for use in reporting the project findings.

## 4. Discussion of Key Findings

The discussion questions developed for face-to-face discussions can be divided into five general topical categories:

- the degree of dependency of the various communities on the oil and gas industry
- the perceived benefits received from communities' close involvement with or proximity to oil and gas activities
- local concerns about the strong presence of the industry along the Texas Gulf Coast
- the public's general perception of the industry, including the quality of communication between the community and industry officials
- the appropriate role for the federal government to play in dealing with local oil and gas issues

The following discussion of key findings is organized around these subject areas. We have made it a priority to provide numerous verbatim quotations from respondents to substantiate our conclusions in this presentation of key findings. The source of specific quotations is provided at the end of the text of the quote. The social sector group of the respondent (B = Business Sector, E = Environmental Sector, G = Government Sector, M = Media Sector) is followed by the name of the county in which the respondent was located.

## 4.1. Community Dependency on the Industry

In a global sense, all of the communities located along the Gulf Coast in Texas – indeed throughout the entire state – are dependent upon the oil and gas industry to a certain degree. As one respondent put it: "Oil is everywhere, and oil is King in Texas." While all of the communities included in this study continue to deal with local problems caused by the industry's bust cycle in the early 1980's, social and economic recovery in some areas is further along than in others.

When asked about the current degree of dependence of their communities on the oil and gas industry, most respondents drew comparisons between their situation now and what they experienced in the 1970s and 80s. It would be difficult to overstate both the positive impact of the industry on this region and the hardship that resulted from the fall of oil prices in the "bust" of the early 1980s:

> It [the early 1980s] was a disaster. A lot of people were broke... restaurants and stores closed down. Real estate dropped 50% – it still hasn't recovered at all. The economy got to where it's very strong now, primarily because there's more discretionary money in other communities that build here and retire here and own a second home here. But...all of the South Texas economy is driven by two things: agriculture and oil. (G – Aransas)

> When you've got the largest complex in the country, and the city is, say, 40,000 or 41,000 population, I don't know how many people are employed by the petrochemical industry, but I would say that probably, just off the top of my head, just a rough guess, 5,000. And if you count their families, you're talking about 15 or 20,000 people – half the population is dependent directly. And the other[s] dependent on them for grocery stores and restaurants. I'd say 90% of the people in Texas City are dependent upon petrochemical. (G – Galveston)

> Texas City would be a ghost town without the oil and gas industry. (B – Galveston)

> We grew up largely as an industrial base for the industry...It really put Houston on the map.... That's what led, though, to the dependence – not only was it the manufacturing sector, it was all of these other sectors that were very much dependent on the oil and gas industry, and as a result of that we lost over 220,000 jobs during the depth of the recession. So our dependency on the energy sector has diminished considerably. However, it is still the most dominant and most prominent industry sector in this region – still very much a major player in Houston. (B – Harris)

> Our tax base has finally reached what it was in 1985. We reached it.... It took twelve years to get back – twelve years. (G – Harris)

This area is very dependent on it. Has been for years and years and years. We're tied to it. And the problem with that is, any change that hurts that industry hurts us, from an economic standpoint.... Any variable that would affect a company would affect us.... And because so much of our economy is predicated upon the petrochemical industry, it could be drastic. Which is, in my mind, the obvious reason that we need to diversify. (B – Jefferson)

The reason Pt. Arthur is in existence... is the oil and gas industry.... Spindletop came in and Texas Oil Company and Gulf Oil were formed in Pt. Arthur.... So our dependence has been throughout this century basically on oil. Up until the 70's, I guess, one of the slogans in town was 'The City That Oils the World,' because about 10% of the refining capacity in the world was situated right here south of town. (G – Jefferson)

I don't think we're nearly as dependent on the oil and gas business as we once were. I think people realized we had a lot of eggs in one basket. I think we learned a lesson. That doesn't mean if we took another real big downturn that we wouldn't be hurt, but I don't think we'd be hurt nearly as bad as the time before because people have long memories. They're not going out and borrowing money. They're not going out and spending frivolously. We learned a lesson, but at the same time, we'd still welcome any increase in the oil and gas. (G – Nueces)

[In 1986], many, many people in Corpus Christi found that they were in the oil and gas business. They just didn't know they had been in the oil and gas business because they were either selling real estate to people who were employed by the exploration firms, or the people doing business with the exploration firms. The hotels found that they didn't have near as much visitor industry as they thought they did. What they had was a whole lot of people flying into town doing oil and gas deals. And suddenly, their occupancies fell off. The real estate industry went into the soup. There was an absolute buyers' market for homes and residential real estate. (B – Nueces)

While all of the communities included in this study are affected by oil and gas, the type of involvement and degree of current investment in industry activities varies across the region. The cities that are most heavily invested in downstream industry activities (e.g., refining and petrochemical production) such as Houston, Corpus Christi, Texas City, and most of the cities in Jefferson County, are the most directly dependent on oil and gas for their continued existence. The majority of employment opportunities in these cities come from either refining and manufacturing jobs or from satellite industries that serve the energy sector. Beyond employment, the economies in these cities are heavily dependent on the tax revenues (both property and ad valorem) that they receive from the oil companies with operations in their area.

The communities that have invested heavily in tourism, such as Galveston, Port Aransas, and Rockport, are less directly tied to the industry, but remain dependent upon the money it generates, particularly in the areas of real estate, retail sales, and recreational expenditures:

Some of the effects are very indirect. Well – the real estate market is probably affected by the turns of fortunes in the oil industry. It bottomed out in the 80's. We're doing better now – there's increased oil business right now. It increases retail business when it's good; it decreases when it's bad. (G – Aransas)

A lot of the people who came here to play were in the oil and gas industry. I don't know how you socioeconomic people look at that, but it is a big factor, because they bought homes for the weekends to play, and they came here in their big airplanes to our little airport out there... they had great big airplanes out there all the time coming and going. That affects your economy. (G – Aransas)

Oil and gas people were a major factor in the development of Rockport because it was a place to come for recreational purposes...that's still true, but not to the extent of the 'good old days' everybody talks about. (G – Aransas)

The synergism of the oil and gas industry and the building industry and the money that's generated out of Houston generates discretionary income if these people want to go somewhere nice and it's close. And nice and close is Rockport. (G – Arkansas)

The indirect affect of the oil and gas business – and I think that people in the industry are naturally risk takers and things of this nature – is that their employees are that way. A lot of them will have second homes down here. And so when the oil business is good... these folks are more than likely going to be buying second homes down here. And so, we depend on that extremely good feeling in Houston of oil and gas possibly looking good. It has affected our real estate market here. (G – Galveston)

I think the business probably brings a lot of people to our area.... All the offshoots of the industry probably bring a lot of people to the South Texas area which, in turn, naturally converts some of those people to buyers and recreational users. (B – Nueces)

When the big oil industry was in full gear and all those people had a lot of money to spend on second homes – in that respect, the economic impact was fairly substantial. (B – Nueces)

The general point here is that the tourist-oriented communities along the coast are dependent upon regional residents having discretionary income to spend, "to play," or to buy second homes in tourist areas. While it is difficult to ascertain exactly how much of this spending comes directly from people in the oil and gas industry, a certain percentage is inevitably linked because the entire coastal area is heavily affected by the presence of the industry in the region. There are also many retired people who have settled in Rockport and Port Aransas, and many respondents indicated that a fair number of these people were retired oil and gas executives.

9

There is a certain degree of dependence on the oil and gas industry in all of these communities, but nowhere is it as high as it was prior to the oil bust in the 1980s. Even in places were the industry is still very active, there are fewer opportunities for local residents than there were in what some respondents called "the good old days" of the 1970s and early 80s. For instance, because of organizational changes within the industry, most companies can now operate with fewer employees. Corporate mergers, increased automation in the refining plants, and general downsizing have all created a context in which most companies have been able to reduce their payrolls. This trend has created a great deal of local concern, and will be discussed in more detail in other sections.

The amount of social and economic recovery that has taken place in all of these communities is most often attributed to local efforts to diversify, and thus to reduce local dependency on the oil and gas industry. In general, no one we talked to expected the industry to ever return to its prior activity and profit levels. The goal for many cities, then, has been to reduce their dependency on the industry by investing in alternative areas. For instance, the cities of Galveston, Port Aransas, Rockport, and Corpus Christi to a lesser extent, have committed to developing tourism as a mainstay for their local economies. Beaumont, Port Arthur, and surrounding communities in Jefferson County are counting on the construction and maintenance of several new prisons in the area to provide jobs, increase local spending, and reduce their presently heavy dependence on oil and gas. The city of Houston has also had economic diversification as a priority over the past few years and has successfully lured non-oil and gas related companies to the city. This priority on diversification as a means of reducing local dependence on the oil companies is reflected in the following quotes:

> If something did crash, we'd certainly feel it, but we're really hanging our hat more on tourism now. It used to be shrimping and tourism and oil. And…shrimping and the oil were the big ones and tourism was just something that would come in. And now, tourism has jumped on top of everything. (G – Aransas)

> There's been such a push to get away from the dependency on oil and gas.... I think people are very reluctant, very cautious when it comes to the oil and gas industry because they've gotten killed by it before. And so, the diversification is there. (G – Harris)

> The tendency is diversification – getting more and more industries coming in – like biomedical research. We're having more of that. We're having more technology coming in. We're having more light industrial companies coming in. More telecommunications seem to be coming into the area. So most of what you've seen within the last years has been in other industries. You're seeing the oil companies downsizing.... There's a sense that somehow or another a lot of other industries are coming into the Houston economy, and that's welcome. The international sector is also welcome. (G – Harris)

> I think we have to realize that it's not going to get any better. It may get worse.... Even with the increase in activity. I mean, I don't think it's ever going to be like

it was. As a community, we're going to have to understand that and go pursue whatever alternative we can to maintain business. (B – Jefferson)

The decline of the oil industry in the 80s – our community has suffered seriously from a loss of jobs and a decrease in tax revenues, etc. So I guess we describe ourselves as having put most all of our eggs in one basket and now we're looking to diversify. (B – Jefferson)

Houston is not as dependent as it used to be – the oil companies have downsized and the city has diversified. People who live here don't think of it so much as an 'oil town' anymore. (M – Harris)

It [the bust in the 1980s] was a truly traumatic experience for the community. I guess we saw that in the way some of the institutions reacted. In 1986, the city formed what was then the Corpus Christi Area Economic Development Corporation. And they had a city commission that was charged with going out and recruiting industry, doing things to try to grow the economy.... Suddenly, people put a far greater emphasis on economic development and economic diversification than they ever had before. (B – Nueces)

In the mid-80s when everything just fell down the tubes, both the city and the individual homeowners and the individual condominiums and the RGC and all those people realized that the money, the buyers, had to come from somewhere besides the state of Texas. So, they just completely reversed all their marketing efforts...they dropped the prices, but not the rates for wintertime and really started directing all their mass advertising to the Midwest.... [So that was your style of diversification – not to change the goods, but to change the marketing?] Exactly. And it's been very successful. (B – Nueces)

The only industry we have in Port Aransas is tourism. That's it. We're not zoned for any other type of industry and over 99% of our establishments on the island depend totally on tourism. (B – Nueces)

In many cases, these efforts to diversify have been fairly successful (although it is interesting to note in the last quote above that Port Aransas has not actually "diversified" – they've simply moved from being primarily dependent upon the oil industry to being almost totally dependent on tourism for local revenue). Several people commented on the fact that Houston is not perceived as an "oil town" anymore, and the construction of prisons in Jefferson County has created an alternative to the areas near-total dependence on oil and gas. The fact of the matter is, however, that all of these communities remain very closely tied to the oil and gas industry. Often those respondents who emphasized diversification efforts followed up these comments later with an admission that oil is still the mainstay in their local economies:

Forty percent of our economy [in Houston] is really oil and gas based. It's diversified incredibly since the late 80s when we had a downturn.... But when you think about the fact that 40% of the economy is still based on oil and gas, that's a significant part. There's no ifs, ands, or buts about it. (G – Harris)

Our dependency on the energy sector has diminished considerably. However, it is still the most dominant and most prominent industry sector in this region...still very much a major player in Houston. (B – Harris)

1985-86 was our worst time. But everything that we can look at that has really influenced our economy has had something to do with the petrochemical industry for the last 90 years. Every five to ten years we always go through a big discussion about diversification. "We can't depend on the petrochemical industry. We've got to get something else." And the thing about it is, they are still our major industry. They're still out there. (G – Jefferson)

We are probably trying to do more diversification in employment over the last eight or nine years than we ever have, but we're still pretty much heavily dependent on the industry. (G – Galveston)

I think it's [Corpus Christi] pretty heavily dependent on oil and gas activity. And spin off companies, and the refining of it here, the jobs it creates – the construction jobs as well as the refining jobs.... Of course, the Port of Corpus Christi – while we're trying to diversify to some extent, probably 75-90% of the cargo that comes in is oil-related, in the refining and petrochemical business. We do a lot of agriculture, but I think over the years, the petrochemical and refining business is a bigger percentage. We're trying to diversify a little bit. (G – Nueces)

This continuing state of dependency is especially true for the region's ports. The ports of Houston, Corpus Christi, Texas City, Beaumont, and Port Arthur are among the busiest in the nation, measured in terms of cargo tonnage, and the vast majority of cargo moving in and out of all of these ports is oil-related. The importance of ports in cities heavily invested in downstream activities has also increased in recent years as more and more of the raw products used in the refining process are imported, rather than domestically produced.

Although there was general agreement about the positive aspects of diversification as a means to reduce local dependency on the oil and gas industry, this opinion was not unanimous. Some respondents thought either that the industry was so entrenched that significant diversification was impossible, or, in some cases, that it didn't even make sense:

I don't think you ever take the place of the petroleum industry here.... It's entrenched. It's 80% of what makes the city go, I would say. (G – Galveston)

The petrochemical industry is here to stay. And this part of the state is going to be that way. (E – Jefferson)

There's never going to be a time in this country that I can see – and I know in my lifetime – that it won't be somewhat dependent on oil and gas. It's going to, so we've got to do all we can to balance the environmental concern with just being able to give the ability to do business in America and do it where they can at least make a profit. (G – Jefferson)

Oil and gas is an important part of the community... and in my perception of this community – heavy industry is accepted. We still actively and aggressively solicit industrial investment here as a community.... Our economic development commissions are still seeking that sort of industry. (G – Nueces)

What we happen to have is a large refining and petrochemical industry because it must have been natural for the industry to locate here. There must have been economic advantages or physical advantages for that industry to be here.... Diversification means to stupid people getting things that they probably can't have. Having business, I would say, the biggest opportunity to develop business in our area involves first expanding that which is already here. And second, going downstream from those businesses.... Energy should be put into keeping the fit geographically and economically. (B – Nueces)

It may be that the degree to which many of these coastal communities can achieve true economic diversity is inherently limited, given the history of the area's heavy dependence on the industry throughout this century.

One final insight about the Texas coastal region's dependency on the oil and gas industry involves the idea that this state of dependency is not always one-sided. For instance, although communities that rely heavily on refinery plants feel threatened by the possibility that a local refinery could pick up and move, one respondent in Texas City noted that this fear was largely unfounded because of what it would cost the companies to relocate. Not only would it be very expensive to transport the massive amounts of equipment currently located in coastal refineries, but these companies also enjoy certain privileges, such as exemption from environmental regulations by virtue of the fact that they were "grand-fathered" when new environmental laws were passed. The "catch" is that if they leave now, they have to bring the site up to current environmental standards, which would be extremely expensive:

I think the industry realizes that they need the community, that they need to be here and operate because they're here and they've got this investment and they need to be able to utilize it. The community needs the industry here to pay for its operations. And so, they both need each other.... If they had to, for instance, shut down their plants, they would have to abandon a lot of equipment because it's not anything you can pick up and move. If you ever look at the stuff, it's piping and blocks. I think Amoco has something like $2 billion in investments in its plants. You don't pick up $2 billion and move it to Indonesia.... And they probably couldn't move to any place in the country – not with the regulations now. A lot of their things are grand-fathered. And they would have to go to a foreign country, which is always a threat. [So, they don't have the freedom to just pick up and take off?] Oh, no. They'd have to leave the plant. Because the stuff is not

13

salvageable. It's not moveable.... Once you've built those things here, they're special custom-built processes and equipment. (G – Galveston)

The argument is that if you don't make concessions [to the refineries] they'll pick up and leave. And this is not so. They cannot leave, because if they do, they have to pay to clean up. And what we have over here is a superfund site. If they left, they'd pay through the nose. So while they might want to leave, they can't. (E – Nueces)

So, the relationship between Texas coastal communities and the oil industry is, at best, an interdependent one, with both sides highly dependent upon continued operations. And while the communities' degree of dependence is not as high as it was 15 years ago, it is still safe to assume that the oil and gas industry remains the primary industry sector in the region.

## 4.2. Perceived Benefits from the Industry

The most significant benefit received from the oil and gas industry in the coastal region is employment opportunities. This category includes jobs for people working directly for the oil and petrochemical companies as well as jobs in support industries that serve the energy sector and, even more indirectly, employment in tourist areas. Cities that host refineries and petrochemical plants, such as Texas City, Houston, Beaumont, Port Arthur, and Corpus Christi, are particularly dependent upon the industry for local employment:

Texas City grew up as an industrial town. The base of our tax structure and our employment structure revolves around the plants.... We are probably trying to do more diversification in employment over the last eight or nine years than we ever have, but we're still pretty much heavily dependent on the industry. (G – Galveston)

We talk about the plants being here since the 1940s. And so, people like me, your grandpa, or your uncle, or your brother, or you father, your mother, your sister, your cousin – everybody's been working at the plants. It provides a lifestyle – and you weigh the advantages and the disadvantages, and you just come out ahead, at least in their mind at this point in time.... And they're paying major league salaries, mind you.... If you work enough overtime, you're making $50,000 to $60,000 a year – that's good in that it provides a nice lifestyle. (G – Galveston)

The people, who live here, live here because they have jobs here. Whether it's directly related to petrochemical or not, much of the development of Houston was based on the petrochemical industry. (E – Harris)

We're enjoying some success in recruiting, retaining, and expanding some of these operations right now. And when you look at the quality of jobs, the pay ranges for employees within the industry, it's very, very positive from the industrial job perspective. The [oil] companies can really pay fairly well, relative to a lot of other industries. (B – Harris)

14

Our [refining] capacity here has always had one of the heaviest impacts, probably of all the counties or regions in the country. It affects about everything we do. It starts off with jobs. That's the first thing. (G – Jefferson)

I think it is almost the only source of income in those communities. Most everybody works in the refineries in those communities – they either work for the city, for the school district, or for the refinery. (E – Jefferson)

What we need is the same old basic thing. We need jobs. (G – Jefferson)

We have used it as our primary employment means.so we rely heavily on the industry. We are fortunate in that in our community, we've had the prison systems come in so that's helping to pick up some of the slack. But I would still say that the vast majority [of local employment] is in this industry. (B – Jefferson)

The majority of the people realize that that's how they've made their living. That's how their families survived for all these years. And whether or not they still work there – even if they're retired – they've got kids and grandkids, church friends and so forth that still owe their livelihood there. And while the wages might not be as high as they used to be, they're still a lot better than they can go work for in almost any other place. (B – Jefferson)

A third of us work there. I may be overstating it, but it's a significant employment base. And even more importantly, its significance has expanded because of the relative income levels in that [refinery] area. The best paying jobs that a kid out of high school or a two-year college or a four-year college is going to get in this town is in the industry. (G – Nueces)

It's my view that the oil and gas exploration business is the only significant business in this part of the country that provides entry-level jobs where you can make some money. If you don't know nothing, but you're hearty and healthy and willing to work on a rig and the jobs exist, you can get that work. And there aren't many jobs like that. (B – Nueces)

The Port of Corpus Christi and this community will die without those [refinery] jobs. I would suggest that maybe 60% of all the jobs generated in this community are generated by heavy industries, in and around Corpus Christi. And if you start driving them out, we're not going to get any more. If you start driving these guys out...the best jobs go away. You can have all the tourist industry jobs you want and starve. (B – Nueces)

As several of these quotations indicate, it is not only the number of jobs available through the industry, but also the fact that many of these jobs are higher-paying and offer better benefits than most other jobs available in the community.

In addition to working directly for the industry, many people in these areas work for companies that directly support both the production and refining of oil and gas. Among other things, this category of jobs includes helicopter transport services (which take workers to offshore rigs), communications companies, copper and other supply service companies, construction businesses, machine, tool making, welding and repair shops, pipeline companies, and the trucking industry. The industry also provides business for upper-level jobs in areas such as technology development, petroleum engineering, and geology. The importance of these jobs in the region was repeatedly emphasized in the interviews we conducted:

> We occasionally have rigs come in for work being done – dry-dock kind of stuff down here. I know there's some helicopter companies that work out of Galveston that service the rigs.... And there's some supply – Farmer's Copper and Marine Supply is a big industrial supply. I think they probably do some oil and gas business. I know there was a local businessman here and his grocery store supplied the offshore rigs and things like that. It's not huge, but it's important because it supports the "little people." (E – Galveston)

> The helicopter business – they buy a lot of fuel and also fly a lot of folk in and out of here. (B – Galveston)

> We are still very much oil and gas related. There's a lot of those other industries that are created and, of course, supported by the oil and gas industries – oil field equipment, oil field research, chemical industries and all of the other satellite industries.... I think that's also significant. (G – Harris)

> Obviously, the offshore drilling and exploration work is having a dramatic impact on the basic manufacturers of components that go into drilling activity. As they go into deeper waters, that's stimulating technology development on how to address and cope with the environment that they're drilling in. So we're looking for companies in the greater Houston area to be in a position to capitalize on the growth of that market. (B – Harris)

> To the extent that these companies are international and they have resources – global resources – obviously, it's very good to have the decision-makers in the community. Because when you have the corporate entity and you have all their key purchasing functions managed and controlled from Houston, it creates the synergy for this city to be a focus for world suppliers of products to the companies coming in. (B – Harris)

> One of the biggest things about this industry – especially on the manufacturing side – if you start looking at refineries and chemical plants, your job multipliers are among the highest of the industry sector. For every direct job that you have in a refinery and a chemical plant, your indirect job multiplier is five or six to one.... If you looked at all the contract maintenance at those huge complexes – the machine shops, motor rewindment shops, the transportation logistics, the pipeline

companies – they touch so many other people and services and support activity. (B – Harris)

As things change, now we're beginning to see things come back in our satellite activities that do relate to whether or not the refineries are doing well. We've got several smaller companies [that] depend on that industry specifically.... They're not what we call major employers, but we've got a lot of them, and that's what our economy really is based on – all of these people. That's where we've come back.... As it comes back in – as an industry it becomes normal – then it will flow in and it will affect other people who aren't out there drilling, but they're support. They're the service. (G – Jefferson)

It's just amazing when you think about it – how many people in the community are involved in the industry. And if you add in all of the support industries, and auxiliary, it would probably be difficult to find anyone in the community who is not. (B – Jefferson)

You've got all your equipment that's used on [rigs]: your valves, pumps, and engines. There are service industries that come into that. You've got electricians that are always involved in that. I've got a couple of friends that spend a tremendous amount of their time going offshore to do work on those platforms and out at the refineries, either working on the generators or whatever else they might need out there from an electrical standpoint. And then you've got your construction business and maintenance business that goes out and works on those things – and expansion contractors. (G – Nueces)

A new rig in the area is a big deal. Each new rig means, depending on the size of it, means a lot of new jobs, 24 hours a day, seven days a week. You've got the rig crews, the logging crews, the trucking people, the tool people, the mud people. You've got a lot of people involved in making that whole [business work].(B – Nueces)

There were lots of entry-level welding jobs, just to give you an example, in the oil and gas industry, which have been gone ten years or more. Now we're seeing a revival of some of that, and we're getting a new generation of workers, because the old generation either had to do something else to live these last ten years, or go.... With the lifting of the market, we've seen a lot more activity of mud companies, pipe sellers, landmen. It's been a significant new business addition.... geologists, landmen, petroleum engineers, and those people – the professional side – and the deal makers. Those guys are finally making a living again. (B – Nueces)

Other respondents emphasized employment opportunities that were not directly linked, but still dependent upon the industry. Most of these jobs were supported by oil company employees who had money to spend on general services in the community:

If they've got good income, disposable income, then they're going to go out and buy cars and clothes and go to movies. A good indication is that for a town this size, we've got a tremendous number of restaurants.... I'm amazed that all the restaurants can stay open. (G – Nueces)

Part of that spin-off is that these folks need automobiles to be driving around and checking on their wells here in town and out in the country. So, you've got your automobile sales, and then, of course, you need people to repair those vehicles and the people who clean them. It's not just the people who are refining the oil and gas who are making the money. Everybody gets a piece of the pie. (G – Nueces)

There's a hotel that's close to the airport where the petroleum helicopters work out of, and I'm sure we get benefit from that. Say they're going to have a crew change...and it gets fogged in, and the employees are here. I think they put them up at that motel until it clears to ship them out there. So those are benefits you get. I think you get housing – temporary housing – benefits from them. Of course the restaurants and those kinds of things.... Galveston is a staging area. (B – Galveston)

I'm sure there are some benefits we receive in Galveston from the people that work offshore. Maybe their families come down here and spend a couple of days with them when they fly off or come back. [It may help the tourism market?] Yes. They could say, 'Well, I'm going to fly out. Let's go down a couple of days early and spend some time together on the beach with the kids, and then I'll leave on Sunday and you all can get home.' I'm sure there's some of that going on, so we derive that benefit from it. (B – Galveston)

I wonder about competition and what happens to Texas City if the plants do go away.... Or what happens to the workers if they decide to go on strike again? ... What that would do, not only to the people that were on strike, but then to all the people who depend of those people that spend their bucks here in town – the grocery stores, the car repair businesses. It becomes so dependent in one direction that it seems like the potential collapse would be pretty heavy if something happened to the jobs. (G – Galveston)

For each plant job, seven other local jobs are created – teachers, retail sales, and support for community enhancement projects. And people coming to work temporarily at the plants fill up the local motels, buy gas, food, use restaurants, cleaners, and other local services. (B – Galveston)

In addition, all of the areas dependent on tourism feel that their local services remain viable largely because so many people in the area make money working for the industry or for satellite' companies. Some of these cities and towns also serve as "bedroom communities" for locations where industry involvement is heavy. Therefore, even if there are fewer oil-related businesses located in places like Rockport or Galveston, many residents live in these locations and commute to other cities to work in jobs that are supported by the industry:

We're so close to Corpus Christi – we're 30 minutes away. We're 20 minutes from Ingleside. All of our towns are 10, 15, 20 minutes away. Our people work in all those towns. What I'm saying is that among the people who work, probably 30 to 40% of them are in some way tied to oil and gas. (B – Aransas)

There's a lot of commuting, even from Houston. People commute, and work four days in Houston and come down for the weekends. They even have second condos that they go back and forth from. And I think it's related to oil and gas. (B – Aransas)

I would say that [the oil industry] has an impact across the county. Of course, Texas City feels most of the impact from that. I know there's other cities that are prospering because of just the employees out there. I know a little community... just 10 or 20 minutes away from here that is experiencing a big boom in construction and houses – home construction out there, because a lot of people that are working here are making decent money and are now moving out there. So you have other communities. You have a lot of support industry in Texas City, but some other support industries that are outside of Texas City. (E – Galveston)

Lots of people live in Galveston and commute to Houston or Texas City to work in refineries or petrochemical plants there. So there is less oil industry in Galveston proper, but the residents are still dependent because they commute to nearby places everyday to work. We really do have a regional economy down here. (E – Galveston)

Much of the entire employment sector on the Texas coast, then, is active because of either direct or indirect ties to the industry.

The second most frequently mentioned benefit of the presence of oil and gas in this region was the tax revenues that local communities receive from the companies. A small percentage of tax money comes from active on- and offshore wells, but most is from property, sales, and local ad valorem taxes in areas where oil companies have large complexes of refinery and petrochemical plants. All of the support companies discussed above, of course, also pay taxes to the cities and counties in which they are located. One of the prime benefactors of these revenues are the local school districts, which thrive when the industry is doing well, and suffer when there is a slump in activity or production. In many of these communities, the oil companies are the largest contributors of tax funds in the county:

Amoco and its sister companies are the largest taxpayer in Galveston County – in their value and the amount of tax that they pay. So, their economic success or continuance here has a big effect on the school district. And, of course, Texas City is one of the school districts in the Robin Hood deal that actually sends money to other school districts because they collect more than what the state says they need. (G – Galveston)

19

The base of our tax structure and our employment structure revolves around the plants...and when I say tax dollars, I mean both a dependency on their ad valorem tax, because they own a lot of property, and also on their sales tax because they have a lot of materials. (G – Galveston)

It gives us a good tax base. Our residents have a pretty small portion of the overall tax burden here in Texas City. It has been estimated that the industry provides about 80% of the ad valorem tax base. So, we as residents have a reasonable tax structure for our homes. As a result of having that much money available, we have a wealthy school system. We have a nice infrastructure within our city. We are able to do a lot of things and have a lot of things that other cities are not able to have. (B – Galveston)

They contribute – I don't have the figure – probably 70 to 75% of the tax base in our community, so we rely heavily on the industry. (B – Jefferson)

The school district boundaries went out as far as, I guess, the law would allow – however far you can extend the school district boundaries to include the offshore wells. And for years when the oil and gas business was really booming...that was their main source of revenue. (G – Nueces)

Our local government knows that they are the largest taxpayers in the community. A significant portion of our tax base is headed by the industrial development down here. (G – Nueces)

Some cities have worked out "in lieu of" agreements with the oil companies operating just outside their city limits. These agreements are basically a trade-off: the city agrees not to annex the land where the company's plant is located in exchange for the company's paying them approximately 70% of the tax money they would have to pay if they were within the city limits. These agreements seem to work well, especially in Jefferson County:

From a financial standpoint, Mobil is not even inside our city limits. But... they make a contribution to us in lieu of taxes each year. And we can provide them some fire protection and very limited services. Mobil, if they were inside our city limits, would be about a third of our tax base.... We say that we have never been at odds with Mobil. We have not. We recognize that they're the entity that gave us, in addition to what our calculations would have been – it's about $5 to 7 million. (B – Jefferson)

The extraterritorial jurisdictions which most of our refiners fit into is actually physically outside of the city limits. And rather than be annexed by the city, the city and the industries negotiated an in-lieu-of-tax agreement. In other words, they're paying the city not to annex them. They're willing to pay a certain fee for services of sorts and being on the outskirts of the community because the city has a legitimate right to annex those companies.... The city doesn't provide full service to those companies because most of them have their own fire protection,

20

water treatment plants and so forth, but they pay that tax at a lower rate because of those factors. (B – Jefferson)

About 60% of our tax revenues come from our in lieu of tax contracts with the industry that is outside of our city limits.... [They pay] about 70%. Really, our ideal answer is don't annex them, but change the agreement where it's not appraisal value. We've done that with Fina. We now have a five-year agreement with Fina that is not based on appraised value.... It's just an agreement: "If you will not annex us, we'll pay you X number of dollars per year and you don't tax." And that's what we're hoping that we can do with some of the others and get away from the tax base appraisal.... I think it's a good solution. Fina seems to like it and we like it. They know what their costs are going to be for the next five years. And we know what we're going to get out of them for the next five years. And we have an agreement on what services are provided each other during that period of time. (G – Jefferson)

The primary motivation for wanting to get away from appraisal-based taxes in this area is that several suits have been filed in the last few years where companies have contested their appraised value and have refused to pay their taxes. The end result is that the cases are tied up in court and the cities are suffering from the loss of tax revenues. This situation has created ill will as well as financial hardship in the communities, and the city governments in Beaumont and Port Arthur have increasingly turned to in lieu of agreements, rather than tax appraisals, to ensure that the oil companies come through with significant financial contributions to the city. The companies comply because their payments under these agreements are significantly less than what they would otherwise owe in taxes. In general, this approach seems to encourage cooperation between industry and city officials and is beneficial to both.

Another factor in taxation of oil companies on the coast is that most cities which host large refinery and production complexes offer sizable tax abatements to the companies. The abatements are negotiated with individual companies, which make exchange agreements with the city government. The offer of an abatement, then, becomes the city's biggest card to play in insuring that the city receives various benefits from the industry:

As we compete more and more in the global market, where there's less government interference, where there's less tax structure...that concerns me. Have we become so dependent on the plants? When do you sell the farm? That's a long-range socioeconomic thing that I look at. [And where do you stand on that right now?] Well, right now, we have developed a tax abatement incentive program where we don't give them the sink yet, but we do [offer them a percentage discount].... And it's based on new jobs created, amount of investment, commitment to local vendors – minority vendors. It's got a whole package. (G – Galveston)

We continue to be fairly liberal about our abatements. We kind of feel like if it offers employment and so on – the sales, the franchise licenses, and so on – then we can offer that. (G – Harris)

Our feeling is if we can get the groups [companies] in here, the fact that they're creating jobs or spending money locally to buy goods and services that [tax abatement] is just one of your competitive tools that you can use to try to attract people here. The offset is create more jobs. Part of the abatement program that we have is geared to the size of the expansion project and the level of abatement. For instance...if there's going to be an abatement,...there has to be a commitment of X number of jobs created – new jobs. Because we want to make sure that we get something in return for giving up the tax revenue from it. And while we understand through the competitive bid process and others, you try to keep your costs down, but there's real emphasis, too, on spending money locally for the construction, and the materials needed in the construction.... I think they're sensitive to that because, chances are, they're going to come back for another expansion, and if we see that they've kind of gone along with what we like to see, that certainly helps the consideration the next time. (G – Nueces)

Again, the abatement arrangement appears to be mutually beneficial to the industry and the communities in which they are located.

Beyond employment and tax revenue, another benefit of the oil and gas industry's strong presence in the area is that the companies and their employees do make various contributions to local groups, projects, and charities. This level of involvement in community affairs is lower in some places than it has been in the past, but is still a significant benefit that offsets some of the liabilities of having the industry so dominant in the region:

The major industries here are very cooperative. I think that here in Texas City we have a unique situation. These industries band together and work on a lot of committees and on a lot of useful civic-type activities. One, for example, is: through the Chamber of Commerce, we have an Earth Day event each year. And we've heard from other areas around here that industry – that they're at each other. They can't work together to pull off an event like that. They're competing with one another, and our industries here pull together. We pull this event off – we have 1,000 people at the event each year. They're very cooperative amongst one another and with the members of the community. (G – Galveston)

The company's employees offer a lot of volunteer support in the community. They contribute to the United Way, get involved in the county fair and rodeo, support the Chamber of Commerce Little League program, are volunteer firemen, provide leadership in churches, schools, city and county government, and participate in the Rotary Club and Kiwanis. Industry people are tremendous corporate citizens. (B – Galveston)

The people that are running these plants in the community live in the community, and they're raising their kids in the community...the people that I know running the companies today are people that are concerned about this community. They're involved in everything, stuff that they don't have to be involved in – about trying to make this community better. (G – Jefferson)

22

They make contributions to the arts, to the social fabric – and it will be sizable to the community. I mean, it's significant. We would know it if they failed to do it... I think they're far more sensitive to the fact that while they're big business, they also are major contributors to all parts of the community and they're trying to handle it in a sensitive manner. To where they're not trying to dominate it – they just want to be a part and they want to make a contribution. (G – Jefferson)

Mobil is very big in the community in terms of money. They give money. Their big thing is education. And so, they've donated money to the school district for certain projects – excellent sorts of projects. And they have a good record in the whole U.S., actually. (E – Jefferson)

Those people are extremely active. They make a concentrated effort to look at ways they can help the community because they realize that the community has relied on their industry for years and years to fund certain things, to contribute to the tax base – greater than any other industry. And where they're having to minimize in some areas, they're trying to compensate by doing things that help the community, maybe at low or no cost to them...they are there for everyday citizens. They are there for school districts. They are there to be involved in whatever capacity they can to contribute to the viability of our community. (B – Jefferson)

They have begun to participate in more and more volunteerism. Leading the way for some community issues that we've had to face, such as crime, such as education, such as economic development, housing, jobs. So all of these things are major issues that the community is concerned with. They have been at the forefront with their brainpower and resources.... They have implemented many volunteers and many volunteer hours for major community service organizations: the United Way, Boy Scouts, Girl Scouts, the Salvation Army.... So in that respect they have done an enormous amount. (G – Harris)

Those community affairs directors not only contribute dollars, but are there actively and physically and working on projects. They support projects with a lot of man-hours. They encourage their staff members at all levels to be involved in the community. (B – Jefferson)

So you've got that kind of organization of the main players in the Houston area, and when you bring them all together, and you have a common problem, and you have some leadership that is more interested in making things happen that are good rather than fighting fights, then good things happen. And I think it's a model for the rest of the country in that respect. (G – Harris)

There are, of course, those who are more cynical about the oil companies being presented as "tremendous corporate citizens." Some respondents saw this as merely "good PR" for the companies, rather than a real desire to help.

Others noted that the companies involvement in the community had decreased in recent years:

They've done some good things with these community groups…and they contribute, at least during the day when they're here, to the United Way, or whatever. I'd like to see some of them living back in the community, and paying their local taxes, and getting involved in the schools and the churches. That would be more participatory in my mind. (G – Galveston)

I think people pay more attention to how charitable a company is – like Compaq. Compaq gives away thousands of dollars every year to schools. Obviously, you and I both know that's kind of a gimmick in itself – you've got them using it at school, you're going to buy one at the house... But I don't think, frankly, [the oil companies] are as out front in giving the big money as they used to be.... It looks to me like they are taking more of a "Southwestern Bell approach" – trying to create a better morale within their own company. (G – Harris)

Now you just don't have the same relationship social-wise. You just don't see these guys now mixing in as much socially, as active in community endeavors. They have a community relation's officer or somebody that's just involved in helping the Chamber or doing work in the school district and all of these things. And they'll give it a little money there, but top management is not involved in it from the major corporations now out here like in Houston… It's just not the same top management relationship, because the managers aren't local people. They don't have a real local knowledge. In fact, of all of the plants in the South County that we have jurisdiction over, there is not one single plant manager that lives in Port Arthur.... That puts us in a little different light. They just don't have any loyalty to Port Arthur. It's not the same top management-wise. A company gives lip service to the community activities, and they give $10,000 here or they give one of the schools their obsolete computers. You know? What is that?… That's a long way from 15 or 20 years ago – if we would've had that same situation and you needed something, they'd sit down and write a $50,000 check out and give it to them. A lot of difference. (G – Jefferson)

In spite of this shift in some communities' relationships with the industry since the 1970s and early 80s, it was apparent from the interviews we conducted that the companies located along the coast do make significant social contributions in some of the areas where they have active operations. One further note about this relationship is that not one respondent living in Corpus Christi in Nueces County mentioned this type of activity as a major benefit in their community. Overall, it seemed that the relationship between industry and the community in Corpus Christi was not as felicitous as in some areas – a point that will be discussed in the following section.

Other benefits that were mentioned included: the boom for local real estate companies when the industry is doing well, the support for tourist areas provided by people who work in the industry and have "money to play," the fact that offshore wells actually provide good environments for fishing, and that the industry provides the majority of the business for local ports in the region. In general, with the exception of some of the environmentalists interviewed, most respondents seemed to think that the benefits of having the industry in the area outweighed the accompanying risks.

## 4.3. Concerns About the Industry

The benefits that communities experienced because of the oil industry's presence in the coastal region were accompanied by some concerns. By far, the biggest concern in all areas was the environmental threat posed by the nature and specific operations of the industry. This was such a major issue that it will be discussed separately from other local concerns.

### 4.3.1. Environmental Issues

The oil and gas, industry is, to some extent, inherently threatening to the environment – spills occur, pipelines leak, drilling requires the disposal of overproduced waters, and refining processes utilize and dispose of toxic materials. All of the respondents in this study recognized environmental threats from the industry and were, to varying degrees, concerned about them. Their major concerns can be placed into four general categories: problems with transport, refining and petrochemical production facilities, beach pollution, and drilling.

In the area of transport, the biggest problem is the threat of oil spills from tankers and barges on the water, pipelines, or rail accidents. A major oil spill would have devastating effects not only on the tourist industry, but could also potentially destroy protected wetlands and bird habitats throughout the region. "Small" spills occur with some frequency, but it's "the big one" that people most fear:

> Our only concern – the only complaint that you'll ever hear by citizens of this county – is: Don't spill anything in the water. (G – Aransas)

> We're a phenomenal birding area. And, of course, a tanker, an oil spill could possibly happen and what if it would happen at the refuge, with the whooping cranes right there? There's only 145--and 200 in the world. What if it were to kill that species? Well then, that's an impact on our economy right there... An indirect downfall for us because we rely on those birds to attract people for tourism. People come from all over the world. They want to come and see the largest bird – the whooping crane. (B – Aransas)

> During Spring Break, the level of attention, the level of concern was really escalated. I would say that from now until the middle of September, people will be more cognizant of the tankers coming in, worrying about an oil spill, what it would do to their business.... The beaches would be polluted and that would just kill the business in the summer. So that's a concern. (B – Galveston)

> Nobody is ever ready for an oil spill. Nobody can be ready. It's devastating what can happen. Look at Alaska – it's going to take years and years and years, no matter how you cut the mustard, to be able to put that back in shape.... We had an oil spill here – I think it was 1994 – that came during our summer season and just

25

turned it off. I mean, it was like turning off a faucet. Nobody came to Galveston. Whether or not it affected the beaches, they didn't come, because the news media hype was so strong – 'Oil all over Galveston!' And it may have been a ten foot patch, but it didn't make a difference. It just destroyed it.... So, spills really have a negative impact. And you can't make up for it, because there's nothing you can do. (B – Galveston)

Obviously, if [a spill] hits a place as tourist-oriented as Galveston is, it would just be a killer. And their economy is so lousy right now that they don't need any storms or spills or anything at all that affects the tourist business, because that would just – I mean, if it just affected a week, a weekend or two, it would have a huge impact on everything. (B – Galveston)

The bottom line is that a big oil spill will kill us economically.... The bottom line in terms of the socioeconomic impact on Galveston Island is that there can not be any spills. We can not afford a big oil spill. And that includes old pipes that are running across the bottom of the ocean, and new pipes, and drilling, and the rigs, and ships going in and off the rigs, and the whole gambit. Bottom line: no spills. We just can't afford it. (E – Galveston)

Just on Monday they had another spill right up the coast in Refugio County, and they first said that there was 5,000 gallons. Now, they're saying there's 1,000 and probably it's somewhere in between. I'm not sure they have any idea how much they really lost in that spill. But the trouble is that it goes into a marshland – lots of people think that marshlands are just ugly places, but actually they're not. They're very productive places. And they may be mosquito-ridden or something, but they're nevertheless the most productive areas that we have. But if you spill oil in a marshland, there's very little that you can really do about it. It's difficult to clean up.... It's marshy and you can't get heavy equipment in there – and besides, if you go in there, what are you going to do, you know? It's in the plants. It's in the soil.... Now, suppose they had the equipment come in – what are they going to do with it? They'd mop it up with a polyester fill, or they'd try sawdust or they try all kinds of things, but then you run into the problem of where are you going to put that stuff? So, you have to have a hazardous waste disposal facility for that material. I don't conform to this 'out of sight, out of mind' scenario, because this stuff is going to enter our environment somewhere along the line. (E – Nueces)

[The refiners] have to bring that hydrogen fluoride in from somewhere. Most of it is coming by rail car from Mexico. You can have a rail accident anywhere. Or it comes in by barge. You can have a barge accident anywhere.... The InterCoastal Canal goes right through the [Aransas National Wildlife] Refuge – right through the whooping crane territory.... And you have either an oil spill or a chemical spill in that InterCoastal Canal...and you have really done tremendous damage. And it's all marshland. There's no way of cleaning it up. We've been lucky. But one of these days, there will be something. So you try to do what you can to prepare for it. (E – Nueces)

Thirty percent of your pipelines are leaking. That's a study – 30%. That's a low estimate. All pipelines – any pipeline put into the ground will leak. I used to lay pipes. I know. It's just a matter of time. (E – Nueces)

We are aware of the extreme possibilities of having oil spills in this area. Just in the five years that I've been here, I know of three incidents with tankers or barges of accidents that, had they been full of some type of crude, it could have been devastating to this area. Because these accidents were right in the ship channel of Port Aransas itself. Of course, all of the barge and ship traffic that comes in out of the Gulf has to come in and go out through here. That is a concern to us because of potential danger not only to people, but also the effects on tourism – of course it affects our tourism, and 95%, of our livelihood is tourism. But it would affect the environment as well. Depending on its severity, it could be short, medium, or long term. (G – Nueces)

From a spill standpoint, if it was severe, and at one of the peak times – say over the 4th of July weekend or Memorial Day weekend, or Labor Day weekend – a period like that where I would normally have in excess of 100,000 people here, it could run 100,000 people away for several days. It could be very devastating. (G – Nueces)

The way the oil industry affects us, of course, is what it could do to our beaches and our marine life. [In what form?] Well, let's take the oil spill last summer – somewhat toward the beginning of the summer. Almost every year I've lived here, we've had someone – whether it's big or small, or a ship breaking in half or whatever – that was carrying their products and it's had a terrible impact on tourism. It's had an impact on marine life and what washes up on our beach and what it's done to our beach.... You have to be realistic about this. We sit right here with a very large port that the ships have to go down the backside of us to get to. The ships come right through our channel right there. (B – Nueces)

One specific issue in the area of transport that was brought up by several people was a concern over the litering process that is currently used in many areas to get cargo from large tankers on-shore so that it can be utilized by the refining plants. Apparently, there have been numerous spills as the raw materials are transferred from the tankers to smaller vessels to be brought in:

Everything is litered in. The LCC, comes in and a smaller ship may make five or six trips into [the refining plant] at the other end of our channel until that whole cargo is in – and they spill out there. They can't help it. It's at night – totally dark. (B – Nueces)

When you have a large number of petrochemical industries and docks, there'll be loading and unloading, and things like that. We've always been concerned about the litering process, and that's a real threat, always, because with all the refineries we have here – they rely on international crude overseas. They're always coming in on supertankers and then just coming up the channel with them. And so there's going to be some bad things that will occur eventually. (E – Jefferson)

Suggested alternatives to this problem include such things as switching to a mono-buoy system several miles offshore or widening port berths so that the supertankers can come further in, but no acceptable solution has been agreed upon by the various interest groups in these areas.

A second major area of concern is environmental hazards created by the refining of oil and the production of petrochemical products. Here the primary problems are air and water pollution caused by the plants, soil contamination, and disposal of hazardous and toxic materials that are used in the refining process. There are major refining and petrochemical complexes in four of the five counties included in this study (all except Aransas County), so there was a great deal of discussion in these interviews about this area of environmental concern. In general, anyone who had been in the area for many years reported that pollution from the plants was much better than it used to be, but that further improvements were needed.

Probably the single biggest destructive force in Galveston as far as the industry is the salt air here. And I think it has been said by others that when you mix the salt air at Galveston with the elements that might be in the air from the refineries,... Galveston is the most corrosive environment in the world. (B – Galveston)

I came to Texas City in 1959.... That was before the real era of environmental controlists – the Clean Air Act and the Clean Water Act were given birth in about 1970. And so, I experienced Texas City before that really happened. And the atmosphere was a nasty place as compared with today. My wife and I lived about 10 blocks from the closest industry,...and it wasn't uncommon for us to hang clothes on the line overnight, and get up in the morning and they'd be covered with soot and the odors. Then, you'd drive into Texas City and, truly, you could see a cloud hovering over the city. Now, that's all changed. It's a credit to the industry. It's probably more of a credit that we as Americans have passed some laws to regulate ourselves, to recognize that we were making an atmosphere that we couldn't survive in.... And I don't mean to say that we've reached the ultimate by any means, but we certainly improved over what we had in the 1960s and 70s.... We have responded to recognize that we were our own worst enemy back there in the 60s and 70s with the practices that we engaged in and we have become much more educated and sophisticated. I think we've still got a ways to go. We've got to keep on plugging, but Texas City has benefited from it. (B – Galveston)

Environmental – of course, that's a big problem. Texas City is a lot cleaner than it was.... 30 or 40 years ago it was really bad, as far as air quality. You could smell Texas City on the freeway. And it still has got some ways to go. It's made a lot of progress, but its still got some to go. (G – Galveston)

In our own backyard here, we have our petrochemical complexes over there in the city of Texas City. And, of course, that's one of our major concerns – the industrial emissions and discharges from those sites.... Our number one priority here at the health district is to respond to citizen's complaints concerning those facilities – air, water, or hazardous waste. All three media, we will look at citizen complaints. [What are those complaints most of the time?] Air side – you get odors, industrial fallout, smoke, dust. Waterside – ...complaints about industrial discharges that don't look good, fish kills, debris in the waterways. (G – Galveston)

We have a community that is surrounded by two chemical plants manufacturing dangerous materials. The problem in Houston is that you've got that all over the place. We really have a lot of chemical industries really close by.... It was a situation where they [residents] were deathly afraid of what was being manufactured in the company and what type of procedures were being used, and safety, and the training and all of these things. (G – Harris)

In terms of the environmental concerns, yeah, there are discharges – they have to burn some off. It's their concern. And it does affect the water. But I think technology is available where they can begin to work through the environmental concerns, it's just a question of time...and money. (B – Jefferson)

They play a numbers game out there. They've got this numbers game, and they say, 'We reduced pollution 25%.' But it's a numbers game. It doesn't mean a damn thing. They're not really doing it. They're just making it look like they are. Easy to do. What we'd like to see them do is get away from these atmospheric flares down there – these big flares in the atmosphere. There's an enclosed flare system that they can adopt and go to. A lot of things they could do, but they've never been compelled to do it.... Sometimes it looks like a war zone out here. It really does. And it smells like the dickens. (E – Nueces)

They've destroyed the bay system. There used to be a lot of oysters by the bay – oysters and clams. There's no oysters at all – they're all dead.... Their air pollutants go into the bay. And they say it's clean, but let me tell you – don't drink it. (E – Nueces)

What we're getting out there is a chemical cocktail. We're getting a few VOC's [volatile chemical compounds] here, a few over there. But when they get into the atmosphere, they don't stay separated. Not one of those refineries can tell you how they interact, if they interact at all. (E – Nueces)

The constant pressure of the odors that emanate from those plants is a problem always. (E – Nueces)

A major problem for Corpus Christi refiners, and to a lesser extent, those in Jefferson County, is that they are being charged with "environmental racism." The environmental justice movement

29

is claiming that because the majority of residents who live immediately adjacent to the refineries are minority group members and/or poor, they are being discriminated against by being exposed to pollution from the plants:

> The problem was generated in the 1960s when the City of Corpus Christi designated what we call refinery row as being an industrial district. The purpose, of course, was to bring in heavy industry. They would be outside the city limits. They would not be taxed like the rest of the city of Corpus Christi is – a tax-free zone, in other words. Now this is fine, provided that you have a long-term vision about where you're going to allow the industries to locate within that district. And this, the city lacked that in the intervening years. They allowed the industry to abut immediately across the street from residential areas. No buffer zone. (E – Nueces)

> If you're going to have heavy industry, the only thing to do is to have a buffer, because people simply cannot live up next to the fence line. And the industries are unwilling to fund it entirely. The city says it's not their fault. Well, it is, because they zoned it. And then they allow those plants even within the zone. They could have said, 'No, you must be at least half a mile away from the fence line.' But they didn't do that. They were so anxious to please the people coming in with industry that the effects on the general neighborhood were just ignored. (E – Nueces)

> It's discriminatory practices because of disparity – the way the population of Corpus Christi is racially distributed. Most people of color are placed near the industry – 78-95% of the minority population is out there.... The city has never tried to do anything about it. It's business as usual. The reason why they do this is people that live near the refineries are people of color. They don't have any clout. They're intimidated to keep their mouth shut. So, the path of least resistance is what it amounts to – the sacrificial sheep. You sacrifice this segment so another segment can live. (E – Nueces)

> I hate to say it, but both the industry and the city believe – they won't admit it, but they believe that these people are expendable. They're poor, most of them. And at least 70% of them are minority of one kind or another.... (E – Nueces)

> What the refineries are telling me is, "We don't want this garbage".... I said, "That's like me going in and taking my trash out of my trash can in the kitchen and saying, 'I don't think I want this at my house,' and taking it over there in their lobby and saying, 'Here – y'all have this,' and not expecting a fuss about it. They're better protected inside that plant than we are outside it. (E – Nueces)

> It's so disgusting.... You just can't let go of it – that there's justice somewhere and we're going to find it.... Probably it has become so adversarial that the refineries say nothing good about the neighborhood and the neighborhood says nothing good about the refineries. It has got to the point where it is simply two

30

divided camps, which should never have been allowed to get to that point.... I don't see a meeting of the neighborhood and the refineries. I honestly don't. What I see is some third entity coming in and trying to get it straightened out, or a catastrophic event happening and wiping out the neighborhood maybe, and there's no one left to gripe. (E – Nueces)

This issue remains unresolved and continues to create tension in these cities between industry, refinery neighborhood residents, and city government officials.

A third category of environmental concerns centers around the condition of the beaches in the coastal region. The cities included in this study that are most affected by this problem are Galveston, Port Aransas, and Corpus Christi. The major problems include trash and tar on the beaches and beach erosion.

One thing that has been a problem...is there has been a terrific amount of ocean trash coming up on our beaches from all of the ships out at sea. And most of those ships are [oil] tankers. (G – Galveston)

When we start talking about the impact of oil and gas in the local economy, it's very easy to begin to look at the garbage that we see on the beach – and some of it clearly arises out of petrochemical production. I have yet to find a tourist carrying a florescent light bulb with them. Hard hats are not common apparel. Some of it clearly is debris that has washed off either inadvertently or on purpose from offshore platforms. (G – Nueces)

The environmental problems we have with the wells offshore is trash. It's illegal for them to dump their trash off the rig. They send these little tugboats out there to change the shift workers and pick up trash, and they're supposed to bring it in. And so, they do try to. But if a bag goes overboard, it just goes overboard.... We do have a major problem from oil tankers... some are conscientious and some are not. (E – Nueces)

Spills are our biggest threat. I think the trash is probably the second biggest issue for us, because we have to spend so much money keeping the beaches clean. And from most of the research, I think they've determined that probably 75% of it comes from the ships and not from people using the beaches. (B – Nueces)

There is another aspect of my interaction with the oil and gas industry, and that is the amount of debris that washes ashore...and a lot of that can be attributed directly to the oil and gas industry. (E – Nueces)

The other thing that we definitely find from the oil and gas industry are items that can only have come from them.... The esoteric chemicals that reek of cleaning solutions, for example, could only have come from there. They have even got a picture of an oil rig on them! The hard hats all have oil company logos, and sometimes there are hundreds of hardhats on the beach. Other things – pipe threads, the plastic thread protectors from the end of drilling pipes that are washed ashore. Rises, which are big collars that go around pipes to add some buoyancy when they need to bring them to the surface – all these things, you can point a finger at them. Pallets – especially pallets – wooden pallets. There are probably more pallets washing ashore than almost anything else. (E – Nueces)

Sometimes if the oil comes ashore, the tar comes ashore in July and August, you can smell it. It's in the atmosphere. I've got pictures of people lying on the beach in their bathing suits and umbrellas up and they're surrounded by tar and trash. (E – Nueces)

... the [erosion] damage is caused by the weight of the ships... ninety-nine percent of it.... Erosion along the channel is a significant problem directly related to the oil and gas industry. (G – Nueces)

The fourth major set of environmental concerns has to do with drilling and production activities. Since the Texas coast is so much more heavily invested in downstream activities, this category of problems did not receive the attention that the three above did, but was mentioned by several people. Examples of these comments include:

They've done a wetlands drill now where if you want to fill in a half acre, you don't have to get a permit for it. So all the little potholes that the ducks used to use for migration are going to be gone, unless we can talk people into leaving them. (E – Galveston)

There's issues that come up with the direct drilling – if we're going into a boom, we're doing more drilling. There are a lot of issues that come up with that in terms of degradation of the environment and being careful. Going out into the wetlands to drill an oil rig, they have to do damage to the wetlands to get the equipment out there.... There are, from what I understand, a number of other problems – for example produced waters... Produced waters is incredibly bad stuff. And so, what we've asked them to do is to build a pit around the oil, around the drilling thing to contain the produced waters and try to pump it into someplace else so that it's not just left to spread all over the whole bay bottom where they're drilling. So, there are things that are issues that the general public knows nothing about that need to be addressed and taken care of. We have no regulations for that. (E – Galveston)

We still have [overproduced waters] as an issue in the Bay. Theoretically, that's not supposed to be going on, or it's supposed to have been eliminated more or less through EPA rules. But there are a lot of people that wanted to be grandfathered in, and there are still a number of facilities that are still pumping overproduced waters into the Bay. Not as many as before, obviously, but that is still going on. (E – Harris)

One particular concern here is the possibility of disturbing bird migrations and habitats in the process of drilling. As one respondent put it:

> There's 20,000 acres in our peninsula here that surround us, and we need them protected. We need them to be pristine and the way they are. Just birding in general is vital to our economy and fishing. We need to protect. (B – Aransas)

In general, respondents recognized that many environmental problems related to the industry were improved over the problems that existed in the 1960s and 70s. However, they also cautioned that some issues had not been resolved and others needed continued improvement. Many credited the industry officials with putting forth efforts to improve their environmental record, but most thought they had only agreed to do this when they were forced into it by government regulations. In spite of the increase in regulations, some companies have found ways to circumvent these requirements. One particular problem is "grandfathering" and other legal exemptions:

> There's a lot of issues over grandfathering and air pollution. A lot of oil plants – they got them to grandfather them out about some of the air requirements. And now, they're finding that 75% of the VOC emissions, and certainly some of the other emissions, are all coming from these grandfathered plants that didn't have to be permitted. That's that. The industry said that the idea was that those plants would be phased out. But they are still with us and they are still producing it. (E – Harris)

> Fifty-four percent of our air pollution is coming from grandfathered, unpermitted industrial sites. Obviously, it must be oil and chemical, because that's mostly what we've got. That's frightening. And we still have all kinds of waivers, the NOx waivers, that we've given companies. (E – Harris)

> We have to eliminate exemptions. One of the things that frustrate us is that we have very little [local] environmental regulation. The one we do have is protecting the sand dunes. Five out of the 20 miles in this county are exempted by statute because they are state parks.... There are two other exemptions in the dune protection act: cattle production and oil and gas. We need to eliminate exemptions. You know, if it's good to regulate this activity for the benefit of the environment, it doesn't make any difference who's creating the problem.... I think we need to apply our environmental regulations uniformly. (G – Nueces)

> One thing [TNRCC] is looking at very closely is grandfathering.... That's one area where obviously there's room for improvement when you have facilities that have been operating with an older technology, and don't have the best available control technology for emissions. There needs to be improvement in float area.... They've talked about moving toward getting a permit and bringing all the grandfathered facilities up to date. (G – Nueces)

Anything as of 3-19-71 is grand-fathered. Pipelines, old rusty pipeline – they don't have to bring it up to standard because it's grand-fathered. They just put that thing in use and use it and it's leaking. (E – Nueces)

Along these same lines, some people were worried about pollution that was created decades before any regulations were in place (i.e., in the 1930s and 40s) and is still affecting the local environment:

It became clear last year that we had some serious ground water contamination in this community as a result of industrial activity, probably in the 40s.... The next big challenge is going to be cleaning up what was done prior to regulation, because some of the contamination we're talking about is not going to disappear.... cleaning up the past, because what we did here in the 30s through probably the 80s has left us a legacy of poison that is going to take a hundred jillion years to clean up. (G – Nueces)

I think one important issue is pollution that has been 'left behind' by the oil industry. I know of one case where Gulf abandoned an old storage pit full of crude oil, the property got sold and was eventually turned into a housing subdivision. The ground water is, of course, contaminated, and now the residents are being affected by it. (M – Harris)

Most respondents seemed to have a lot of faith in the state's ability to respond to oil spills specifically, but there was a considerable amount of dissatisfaction expressed about other environmental regulation agencies. Given that their mandate may be an impossible one to achieve, there is a definite shift among some environmental groups to establish more cooperative relationships with industry officials. Some organizations are also pushing for "voluntary compliance" policies to encourage the industry to monitor itself in some areas. Overall, the interviews in this study indicated that the populations in these coastal areas are very environmentally conscious.

### 4.3.2. Other Concerns

Non-environmental concerns about the strong presence of oil and gas in this region focus more on the ways that the social infrastructures of these communities are threatened by the industry. Some of the concerns expressed were specific to individual areas, while others were more global. Not surprisingly, respondents' broader concerns often paralleled their perceptions about how they benefited from the industry. For example, since the biggest benefit received from the industry was local employment, their biggest concern was the threat of a reduction in those jobs. In response to the downturn in the 1980s, many companies have taken steps such as downsizing their operations, investing in automation, or merging with other corporations to increase their profit margin. These steps have resulted in fewer jobs in the communities where these companies are located. Ultimately, of course, higher unemployment is associated with higher crime rates, higher levels of poverty, and sagging real estate markets:

There's no question – when you have a higher unemployment rate, the crime rates increase. That's national. I mean, it's well known that you're three times less likely to get involved in crime if you're employed.... It's not just [the oil companies], but, of course, as long as they're strong and viable, it reduces, to some extent, our unemployment issues.... It affects the schools. It affects the crime rate. It affects the real estate market. It affects everything that is involved in the community to make it operate. I don't guess there's anything that impacts us more. (G – Jefferson)

One of the uncertainties about when you have a large employer like you do in Texas City like Amoco, Union Carbide, some of the other plants, if you have any little change, it affects a lot of people's lives. And in this day and time, the different acquisitions by one company and another company, and the changing of the products that a plant may produce – you have some of that in Texas City. You've had several plants that I know of that have either changed hands or ownership.... So there's always a change of possible management and middle management. You don't know what they're going to do as to whether the plant is converted to a different process and there's a different employee number. [So the big effect there is whether you're going to have a job?] That's the uncertainty. In other words, it's like a shopping center where you have a Kroger's or Randall's in it – if they ever move out, you're in trouble. If you have just a number of small businesses, one leaving doesn't hurt a whole lot. (G – Galveston)

We're seeing just the corporate downsizing and what's called 'shared services,' which had been here a couple of years ago.... You have Amoco, for example, who is our biggest employer [and has several corporate offices]. Why should each of them have an accounting service? Why should each of them have a data processor? And then, you have Amoco in Houston. You have Amoco in Clear Lake. You have Amoco in Bayou Vista. Well, they finally got smart and they started creating shared services. And that not only calls for reduction in the workforce, but it caused them some relocation, because when you share services, you're going to share them out of one office.... If you do it at that level, then it seems to me the next step somewhere down the line is that they will share services in maintenance. Why have a pipefitter's group in each plant? Why have a welder's group in each plant... That's when you start having, again, reduction in the workforce.... It's a trade-off. We're happy to have them because it's a nice, stable job. It's a good paying job and nice benefits. If that starts to go away, then you have to question whether it's worth it. (G – Galveston)

If you look at the production volumes of these industries out here, the volumes have gone up. The employee count has gone way down. We have fewer employees at these industries now than we had back in the 70's or 80's.... I heard someone say the other day that Union Carbide, for example, had about 800 or 900 currently employed there, when at one time they had over 1,800.... This has always been a heavily blue collar, unionized workforce. There aren't near as many of those blue-collar jobs as there used to be. [Because of automation?]

35

Because of automation and general downsizing and consolidation and economic moves internally. There has also been a move away from unionization, so there is some effect there on the union population. (B – Galveston)

As they modernize operations, they are constantly looking for efficiencies. And one of the things that companies are doing today is using more contract employees. They're using more what they call 'full-time temporaries,' as opposed to permanent-type people, and looking for every way to automate. It's amazing that you can build a $200 million chemical complex and put 125 people to work, and they run the whole darn thing. They have some maintenance people out there, but that kind of investment in any other industries – or a lot of other industries – would be a huge workforce. (B – Harris)

We as a community are going to have to find ways to build our tax base as well as create jobs, aside and apart from the petrochemical industry. The chemical industry, of course, is expanding somewhat, but we're having problems, of course, with the exportation of jobs overseas. (B – Jefferson)

As they've been forced to replace old units that weren't competitive and they couldn't make profits with them – as they've been forced to do that, they replaced them and they're all computer run and they're automated, and instead of having 500 people on a shift, now they have 15. So, you don't have that many people that are involved. And their jobs are not stable. They don't know if they'll be there next month or not…. We don't have enough jobs. Gulf, which is now Chevron – and Texaco, they'd have 2,000 people on each shift. They don't have 500 now. They don't require that. Used to, they'd have operators, back-up operators, watching dials, doing all sorts of stuff. Now they don't do it at all, and besides that, they don't have in-house maintenance. They hire contractors to come in and do things. (E – Jefferson)

The biggest thing that's changed the dynamics is the modernization – electronics, computerization, and all of the things that go with it, because you just don't need the people. That's what happened to us in the town 10 or 15 years ago. Texaco, at that time, before they sold out, they were running a huge refinery out there and had 7500 employees, and when they got through they had 1500 employees. They downsized, but they also at the same time modernized. Instead of having a whole group of men out there called operators that manually run a unit, one guy sits behind a bank of computers and controls and runs it. That's where everything sort of cratered in Port Arthur and Jefferson County and everywhere along the coast…. They spent hundreds of billions of dollars to modernize the refineries, but the flip side of that coin is that you don't have many people to operate it. (G – Jefferson)

In the past, people could graduate from high school, get a job in the refinery, and be set until retirement. Not anymore. After the mid-1980s, when the core industries invested in automation, the available jobs were reduced. The petrochemical workforce was reduced maybe 40-50%. (M – Jefferson)

Another global concern was the uncertainty and vulnerability created by communities being too dependent on the industry. One general solution proposed was to continue diversification efforts.

> We've become lazy in this community and dependent – just thinking that it's always going to be there.... And because we've become dependent on it and haven't been, I think, as foreseeing as we should have been, then we were caught short in the 80s. I still think there's an old-time mentality that it will always be there. But the more I read and the more I travel across the state and this country, I'm seeing that that reliance is unfounded. We're going to have to go out as a community and try to diversify. (B – Jefferson)

> We've got to have more jobs. We've got to do that by trying to get local business industry to expand, but at the same time, bring in related industry that can utilize, for instance, the plastics. We have numerous petrochemical plants in this area that make plastics...and send it somewhere else in the company – they have a plant that makes it into the product that's sold. Why not make some of those products right here and ship the finished product instead of the raw product? ...So I'm hoping that that's what will happen – we'll see those type of development industries invited into our area to help these people find jobs. (G – Jefferson)

> The biggest problem now is getting some more jobs and getting those minorities and those uneducated people educated and working. If we could reduce that 10-12% unemployment to 5 or 6%, it would make all the difference in the world. [But you can't count on the oil companies to do that?] You've got to diversify. We've got to bring new businesses in here that will feed off of those to a degree. Use the products coming out of that plant and make something. (G – Jefferson)

> What we've done is, we started off producing the crude oil and then, natural gas. And then, we've made some initial products from it – fuels, primarily.... And each time, we're trying to reach a little bit farther down the line to get the jobs – they become more labor intensive, the more you get manufacturing toward the consumer... And so, we're kind of doing building blocks. And so, as I like to tell them, we know that is our future, and that's the importance of diversifying even the port. Because there will come a day – we don't know when it is – but somebody will come up with a way to move people around and about in their personal transportation, and they will not be burning gasoline. I want to be refining the last barrel of crude into gasoline, but when that goes away, you've got to have something to follow along. (B -Nueces)

One factor that contributes to the precarious position of the communities most invested in the manufacturing end of the industry is the globalization of the economy, and especially the oil industry. Some companies are apparently threatening to move their operations overseas, where labor is cheaper, and regulations are more lenient:

Basically, my understanding is that it's not unlike what's happening across the nation – because of the permitting processes and those kinds of things, these employers are going overseas. They're just packing up and going other places because of our permitting process and our requirements. (G – Jefferson)

That's a special concern – whenever companies are dealing with international properties. Let's say Shell/Texaco got together on properties that they have in the Middle East or something, and elected to relocate their management team to closer proximity overseas as opposed to leaving their corporate offices here – that's our biggest concern. (B – Harris)

Amoco had applied for tax abatement, and it was a question of: if they didn't get it, they would take their $200 million plant somewhere else. So, that has a lot of effect on what the labor force looks like in this community. (G – Galveston)

The biggest concerns that I see are how we're going to deal with the issues of being in a global economy and knowing that these standards that were passed here aren't passed in other countries... The companies pick up and move. We've got to have something to deal with those issues, and I'm not sure I've got the answers to that. But when we continuously get more restrictive, and more restrictive, and more restrictive, ultimately they're going to move all of our jobs out of the country.... And yet, I would never be an advocate of going to the relaxed standards that they have in Mexico for air quality. I mean, it kills you. There's no question of this. It really is a very, very, very difficult balance. (G – Jefferson)

Ironically, it seems that the same regulations communities have to improve their air and water quality may ultimately drive the companies that are their economic mainstays overseas. However, as was noted earlier, because of the expense of transferring their operations, this may not even be feasible for many refiners.

The communities that were heavily invested in tourism were concerned about any developments in the industry that might jeopardize their dependence on visitors and potential real estate customers:

We're definitely doubling in size when the town is booked with visitors. So anything that would happen that would make occupancy go down would be detrimental to us. Tourism is our major industry. (B – Aransas)

Tourism is quick. You can book a tour group in town and boom – those hotels are full. They drop $30,000 in the community and they're out of here. So it's quick... It's scary if they don't come. (B – Aransas)

I was in tourism – I'm trying to think how many years ago – maybe seven years ago when a ship broke in half right off our shoreline... And I could see the oil everyday. I would stand at my bedroom window and watch that patch get closer and closer. I would go to work and listen to the phone calls, the people calling from all over the United States: 'Is it on the beach? Should I cancel?' And I kept watching that spill get closer and closer, and listening to those phone calls. And I've always known that's how it would happen. I grew up in an oil field, and I also know that there is no such animal as a foolproof blowout. It's not going to happen. (B – Nueces)

Corpus Christi, which is trying to simultaneously attract tourism and industry, has an interesting problem in this area:

One of our targets is becoming a visitor destination. We have put a lot of emphasis since 1986 into expanding our visitor industry. And I've had people ask me, 'Well, is it consistent to have as your economic development targets an expansion in the visitor industry at the same time you're trying to expand port industries [refineries]?' Well, and my answer is if we were talking 50 or 75 years ago, the answer would definitely be no. But today with the Clean Air Act and with the amendments to the Clean Air Act, what we're doing is cleaning up the refining petrochemical industry.... So it's not inconsistent from my view anymore to be able to have the channel port industries located in close proximity to a place that wants to be a visitor destination. But, certainly in people's minds there's still a tradeoff. They drive on Interstate 37 and they look over there and they see a bunch of refineries, and they say, 'Golly, is this what the brochure said?' (B – Corpus Christi)

Communities that are committed to supporting the refining aspect of the industry have general health and safety concerns about being in such close proximity to the plant complexes:

We are a cancer corridor. We have the highest rate of cancer in the United States other than the Mississippi River, which is another corridor of petrochemical companies. Living around this concentration of petrochemical companies is a health hazard. (E – Galveston)

I've got to be more concerned about the health of the community. And it would definitely appear, from what I've read, that here in Southeast Texas, we have a higher percentage of various types of cancer than they do in other places. I doubt very seriously that it's the Big Thicket that's causing that! (G – Jefferson)

Our cancer incidents in this area is terribly high. And people act as if it isn't going to affect them. But the fact is that they die a lot younger. And they often don't live out the years to 65, to retirement. (E – Jefferson)

They have been, in their minds, significantly hurt in long term health, because there are a lot of people who live over there [near the Refineries] who complain of increased asthma, cancers, lung problems of other kinds, skin rashes...so we do have a problem. (E – Nueces)

There's always the risk factor involved around safety at the plants when you live in Texas City. (G – Galveston)

A cataclysmic event like the hydrofluoric acid leak that Marathon had some years back – ten years ago, I guess. It was a pretty good example of the kind of emergency event that would be of concern to us here.... When you think about the flammability of the products that are produced in those places, and a vast volume of them, it sounds like it's a virtual powder keg sitting out there. (B – Galveston)

We had a warehouse fire. And that fire was the factor that got us into the issue of hazardous material storage. The debate then is: how do we regulate it? What kind of safety concerns should we follow? So that particular fire was the company coming in and not giving a second thought to what they were actually putting in these warehouses. (G – Harris)

We put together large volumes of potentially dangerous materials that are flammable or toxic or whatever they may be, and when you do that, you are creating the opportunity [for an accident]. It may not be very big, but the opportunity is there. (B – Harris)

All four major refineries use hydrofluoric acid in their units down there. Pretty bad stuff.... If you ever get a release of this stuff, it's deadly. One inhalation of it and you're dead. And they use thousands of pounds of it out here in the process in the refineries. And we're trying to get them to change to a safer chemical. (E – Nueces)

I honestly believe that we're going to have a catastrophic occurrence with these plants at some point.... And we would have to have that catastrophic event that blanketed Corpus with a deadly gas or hydrofluoric acid or whatever, for the people of Corpus to wake up. (E – Nueces)

There's no question that what you do at a refinery and a petrochemical company is a more dangerous activity than certain types of manufacturing. (B – Nueces)

A couple of people noted that working in a refinery community puts a considerable strain on families, not only because of the uncertainty about future employment, but because of the nature of the work itself:

From a social standpoint, you would talk about the family. And, of course, you get back to the economy – that's where the money comes from, because that's your major employment sector. So it creates a dependence for the families, and also, any of the other service and retail businesses that depend on it as far as their employees, in that that's where their livelihood comes from. And it would probably affect their level and quality of life and certainty and uncertainty as to whether they can plan for their continued style of life. As they would prepare, for example, college education for their children. (G – Galveston)

If you work enough overtime, you're making $50,000 to 60,000 a year. When you talk about socioeconomic, that's good in that it provides a nice lifestyle. It may be bad because to get enough overtime to get to that figure – I think you get a lot of divorces. I think that's one of the side effects that nobody even thinks about. There's a lot of shift workers. It's bound to cause a strain on families. (G – Galveston)

Getting back to the social aspects, I'm concerned whenever you have shift work situations – I'm concerned it will affect the family life. Besides the divorce rate that I was talking about, as you get into longer shifts, we've gotten away from the 60's where we had 8-hour shifts and overtime. Most of them have gone to 10- or 12-hour shifts. The way they compensate for that is now most of them that are on 12 hours want to work 14 days a month. But for your sleep schedule, you look for long chances to where you've got some time to spend with your family, but for the other 14 days you don't see your family. That concerns me. I think if you look, and I don't have any statistics, and I don't know where you would look to get them, but I think we're going to see the participation at the churches way down from what it used to be when I was growing up, just because of overtime and sleep schedules. I don't think that you see young families going to church. And participation in schools, participation at home with your kids with homework – I don't know that we were doing that well. Now, our TAAS scores have gone up, and this last school year, we've had three elementary schools the State recognized for TAAS scores. But I wonder about the family unit and the participation in school, church, and extracurricular activities. (G – Galveston)

Another related issue is that in some of these communities, the residents who live near the refineries are not the ones who necessarily get the most benefits from the presence of the industry, and yet they may get more than their share of the risks. This can create some resentment toward both the industry and other residents:

And I tell you what, the emphasis has changed front the 60's and 70's, and the plants, I think, recognize that. Of course, they had 8-hour days in those times. And to give something back to the community, they made sure that their salaried people lived in town – their managers lived in town. And it was an unwritten rule that you will participate, whether it's Boy Scouts, whether it was church groups, whether it's in Little League, whatever. Well, as we became more of a blue collar town, I think you saw a shift where the plant managers and the upper level managers, and now even the engineers, the upper-level salary people, all live in Clear Lake, or Friendswood, or South Shore, and League City. And you don't get the participation at that level anymore from the plants in making sure that there are these rounded activities – just activities from the plant that you would get from white collars. I think that has changed. (G – Galveston)

It's an 'enterprise zone' – these poor neighborhoods are within the enterprise zone.... Now this enterprise zone doesn't take in the whole city, or county – just the primarily impacted – negatively impacted – neighborhoods. And they're supposed to, by law, hire 25% from these neighborhoods within the enterprise zones. And they don't do it. [It's less than 25%?] Less than 1%. (E – Nueces)

I would say out of 300 families, maybe15 people [work at the plants].... And I really don't think there's 15. I'm being generous when I say 15.... The most I could find from talking to some of the older neighbors was 18% employment in the plants. (E – Nueces)

[Do they hire people who are at risk because they live close?] No. Probably not. But a lot of that is because what you're dealing with is obviously property near industrial settings has fallen in value over the years. It's hard to sell, and so it tends to become middle, lower, and lower income housing. And that tends to equate to lower education levels, and tends to rule them out as employable. (G – Nueces)

That was something else – they felt that these chemical companies were garnering all of their resources in this community – their labor – and taking from the community and not giving back. That's another thing that I think has been in the rhetoric is the amount that business is contributing back to the communities where they are located. (G – Harris)

Finally, there were some concerns that were more specific to particular communities. For instance, in Jefferson County, there is a lot of anger among residents toward some oil companies that have refused to pay their taxes. Apparently, in recent years, several companies have challenged the appraisal value of their properties (established by the county), and some have withheld their tax payments until matters are settled in court. This constitutes a major loss of revenue for the communities throughout the county, and obviously, has created great concern. It is another example of residents feeling that they contribute to the industry, but are not getting back what they should from the oil companies.

Another situation involves the impression among some residents of Corpus Christi that the refineries in the area are putting a serious strain on the city's water supply. Corpus Christi and some surrounding areas are experiencing what one respondent called a "water shortage crisis" right now -- the citizens have been on mandatory rationing for over a year. Industrial sites, on the other hand, have been granted some concessions and are not as affected by the drought situation. This situation has created some suspicions of inequity among some of the people who live in the area:

The city provides [the refiners] water...for their industrial needs. They will use roughly 50-60% of the water that's consumed by our total water usage. Particularly in times of drought, like the last couple of years, that creates a little tension, especially when you're talking water rates.... There's a little tension, because, obviously, people want to make sure they've got enough for their homes and their families. At the same time, you want to make sure the refineries have enough water to keep working, because they employ so many people, and it would

42

have a devastating effect on the economy if the refineries shut down. (G –
Nueces)

Industry has been given all kinds of concessions. They pay much less for water
than anywhere else in the state. They pay much less for water than the citizens in
Corpus Christi, even though they use more than half of the water that comes into
the city.... We've been in a drought... our reservoirs are only 30 and 35% full. So,
the city has finagled to buy water from Lake Texana, which is 100 miles away,
and put in a 60-inch pipeline to bring that water to Corpus Christi. Now, the
water is not needed, in my view, unless you expand the industries, which is what
they want to do.... Now, the total cost to the citizens of Corpus Christi will be
$700 million over 30 years by the time you pay the interest and all this kind of
stuff, and pay for the water, which is expensive water.... Our water rates are going
to go up about six to ten times over time to pay for this. Now, who that hits most,
of course, are the poor. I mean, it's not going to hurt me to pay another $5 or $20
a month for water, but it hurts the poor. And so this is, again, an unfair thing that
is done to people, and quite often, minority people. (E – Nueces)

It is interesting to note that among all of the counties we included in this study, this situation in
Nueces County was the only one in which the industry was seen (by some) to put any strain on
city services – a concern that we expected to be more widespread.

These, then, are some of the major concerns that respondents had about the strong presence of
the oil and gas industry in their communities. The general attitude about risks associated with the
industry was summed up by one respondent who said:

I think that you've always got to be optimistic that, you know, the only reason
why the risks are there is because there has not been a concerted effort of putting
it in check. And I think that's the proper approach. You have to deal with those
risks and you have to put them in the proper perspective.... [And so, ultimately,
the benefits outweigh the risks?] Yeah. Most definitely. I think so. (G –
Galveston)

## 4.4. Perceptions of Community Relationships with the Industry

A fourth goal of the interviews was to obtain information about the general relationship between
the industry and people in various communities along the Texas coast. Some of the questions we
focused on included: How much communication is there between industry officials and the
general public and how effective is this communication? Do the residents feel that they have any
influence over industry decisions and activities? What is the general attitude of the community
toward the industry? Because our sample targeted business and governmental leaders and
environmental activists, we were somewhat limited in trying to obtain this information as it
applied to the general public. However, we did ask our respondents about their impressions of
the more general public's attitude toward the industry, and received some useful information.

There was more disagreement among the respondents on this issue than on any other topic covered in the interviews. Part of this had to do, of course, with the fact that we talked to people in different sectors, having different perspectives and different interests to protect. We conclude that it also truly reflects the variety of opinions and attitudes about the industry among the people who live in communities along the coast. There is no single consistent attitude toward the industry, and the opinions that do exist apparently change over time, depending on recent events.

Several respondents, especially in those communities that are more distant from the industry (i.e., tourist areas), thought that local residents didn't really think about the industry that much, were ambivalent, or even complacent:

> I would say they would be more concerned about tourism and that type of thing – and maybe the shrimping industry.... These guys in here don't even think about the oil business. (G – Aransas)

> It's just things you don't think about. You know, you just go about driving around the streets like everybody else, buying your groceries and raising your kids, and you just don't think about it – unless something happens. (G – Aransas)

> This is an oil and gas state. So many have lived and grew up in it like me. They really don't worry about it. We just feel like they're doing the best they can. I think they do, most of them seem to be reliable types. We don't see it as a big risk, or something to be worried about. (G – Aransas)

> It's not the focus here. It's kind of in the background. Nobody really speaks of it, or it's not heard of. Nobody says anything about it. (B – Aransas)

> I don't know whether the populace is aware of [increased oil and gas activity]. If you were to ask Joe Blow Citizen, 'Do you know that the forecast for the overall industry is improving?' I'm not sure whether they know that.... (G – Harris)

> I would say that the people who live here are oblivious to everything beyond when the next garbage pickup is. I think that's the sickest thing.... They just don't seem real tuned into what they're losing or what's in danger, it's been here so long it's a fact of life. (E – Harris)

> I would say that people really don't look to oil and gas as being a major driving force in what keeps Port Aransas going. (B – Nueces)

> The one thing that bothers me is that we are complacent about industry – about what goes on in these industries. Now, complacent may not be the right word. I think that what it is, is that our citizens have developed a confidence – almost to the point of being complacent. That's not 100% true because we do have some folks that are still very skeptical about what industry does. But I think overall, we have a confidence that industry is watching out for our best interest. [Where did that come from?] I'm not sure. I mean, did it come from the fact that industry has

44

done a decent job over the years?  Has industry brainwashed our people to think they've done a good job when they really haven't?  I'm not sure.  But I have experienced personally, with my clients [oil companies] of course, public hearings.  We put our notice in the newspaper of a public hearing on a permit application, or a community meeting on the [specific issue] – nobody shows up.  Now, is that complacency or is it confidence?  (B – Galveston)

I think if you asked some of the people out there, they would not say something bad about Mobil.  They would probably be closer to being ambivalent.  (G – Jefferson)

When people do think about the industry, they have many different reactions to it.  For instance, some have a very positive, trusting response:

I tend to think that they are far more sensitive to the fact that while they're big business, they also have major contributors to all parts of the community and they're trying to handle it in a sensitive manner.  They're not trying to dominate, they just want to be a part and they want to make a contribution as opposed to trying to dominate....  We've never had a disagreement with them.  If we had, we have been able to work it out.  Because we recognize that our interests are the same.  We want them to do well – and we do well.  And they don't want to damage the community, and we don't want them to.  (G – Jefferson)

I think, generally speaking, communities get good communication, and there's a good working relationship now that's been formed.  (G – Nueces)

The major industries here in Texas City are very cooperative.  I think that here in Texas City we have a unique situation.  These industries band together and work on a lot of committees and on a lot of useful civic-type activities.  (G – Galveston)

For the most part, people think real favorably of the industry because we know that it's done good – it's made our city.  Our city was literally founded through the industry.  You do hear some concerns and criticisms...but I think when you get right down to it and you talk to people about what they think, we all realize regardless of who we are, what area of town we live in, or where we work, that our city couldn't survive without the industry – we would be devastated....  People realize that while they may not be employed there or they may not have a relative right now, most all of the families in our community have come at some point in time from a refinery family.  (B – Jefferson)

I think our industrial sector here is well received by the community.  It is the best paying jobs in the community, and people know it.  Our local government knows that they are the largest taxpayers in the community... and there's a pretty decent feeling they they're moderately protective of the community.  (G – Nueces)

As a whole, the communities support the industry. There's no question about that. They don't want them to leave. The majority of the people understand. There are lots of cities in the United States that would like to have the problem we've got, you know? There's still a heck of a good payroll out there. (G – Jefferson)

Then there are also those who report a "mixture" of feelings about the industry among the people in their community:

[People in Galveston] are going to tell you that there's some good ones and there's some bad ones. (G – Galveston)

It's real mixed. It depends on how you define a 'general citizen.' Obviously, because there is so much petrochemical industry here, there are a lot of people who work in that industry, and they don't think it's terrible. They make their living there. And then, you have a lot of people who think that all that's a pit – that it's terrible and a blight on the face of the earth. And there are people who think that Galveston Bay must just be this horrible cesspool. But then, you have people who recreate on the Bay who know that it isn't a horrible cesspool. So it's a real broad range of perspectives about the oil and gas industry. (E – Harris)

You have a mixture. Most of the community is very supportive still of the industry as a whole, even though they've had a lot of layoffs in the past. There is a group of people, probably the people that live near the refineries, that have always been more or less negative to them, and are more so now in some cases than others. This has rubbed off on one or two members of the [City] Council, and they just think the whole industry is greedy and taking what they want. (G – Jefferson)

Moving on down the scale, some people think that the relationship between the industry and the communities requires some caution:

I don't mind them, because they are trying to follow all the EPA laws. And they've been around a long time. It's just like a bad son in the family. If you have five sons and one of them is not that good, you're going to keep him, you know? They're not the cleanest or the best one you have, but its still part of your community and it has been for a long time. So, we learn to live with those. But...let's say that they weren't here and they wanted to come in here? Not now. They wouldn't be able to get in. We've kind of grandfathered them in, and they're just lucky they're in here. That's the way I would put it. And they might tell us, 'Well, you're lucky we're providing these jobs and stuff, too.' I'm not in a shouting match with them. I just want to let them know that's the way things are now. That's the way they're going to be in the future.... We'll take anything along the way as long as it doesn't hurt us. (G – Aransas).

[Do you trust what you hear from the oil industry officials in your relationship with them?] No.... You do the handshake, but with caution. That's all there is to it.... And it's not speaking badly of them. I'm just letting you know that it's something you've got to watch. You can't just say, 'Yeah, a handshake and let's just go.' Not anymore. You just have to be real careful with things. (G – Aransas)

Next, there is some outright distrust of the industry:

I can tell you this about oil and gas: there is a general perception here that they cheat. They cheat any and every way they can.... The perception of the general public is that they cheat and they dump not only what's permitted (which is bad enough), but that if they have the opportunity to do it and get away with it, they'll dump what's not permitted. Now, whether that's the case or not, I have no way of knowing. (E – Galveston)

They tell us lies and it's obvious they're lying. You know? And then, they'll say, 'Oh, we do that because we reduce our liability.' That's not an excuse for lying. You don't have to lie to run a business. But they do. (E – Nueces)

I think they're frightened to death of making a stir – they will lose their jobs. We know of an environmentalist who...made a fuss about some doings of Mobil, and her husband and her son both lost their jobs. They're very threatening people. It's like the mob. And they bet on the fact, I think, that people just won't leave. They will not leave and look for something somewhere else. They'd rather stay and tough it out and die of fumes and lack of money. (E – Jefferson)

With this range of opinion, it is not possible to characterize the public's "general" attitude toward the industry. There is, apparently, no single relationship between oil and gas and the communities in which they do business. There are a multitude of situations, interests, and experiences that have led to a variety of perspectives in this area. This, in and of itself, offers strong evidence of the impact the industry has historically had on this region.

There is certainly more potential for ongoing tension between the industry and residents in communities that host refinery and petrochemical complexes. The oil companies in many of these areas have attempted to open up communication lines with citizens by sponsoring organizations like "Citizens' Advisory Panels" (CAPs) and by reducing the inherent risks to neighborhoods adjacent to the refineries by helping to pay for "Local Emergency Planning Committees" (LEPCs), which outline specific steps to follow should an accident or emergency occur. Once again, there is a range of opinions about the motivations for, and effectiveness of, these programs. Some respondents thought they were very effective and demonstrated the industry's general openness to the community:

First there is CAPS, the Citizens Advisory Panel – we suggested that a long time ago. We came in – I think it was the 20th Earth Day or something like that – had an environmental challenge to local industries to let citizens have more knowledge and say so as to what went on behind the gates and that type of thing. And a couple of industries agreed to it, and we set up an advisory committee and met. And the Texas Chemical Council came in and said they wanted all their people to do it. And so, right now it's all over the whole state.... We had a lot of Citizens Advisory Panels, and members of our organization are members of those advisory panels. And we would meet monthly or once every two months, and their people from the plant would come and talk to us, and we would talk to them to find out what's going on, when their permits were due. [It's mostly to improve communication?] Communication would make things more open, and if things were open, you would find out these things are done better.... You can't hide things. [What's their motivation to participate in something like that?] It has to be public relations. [The classic image of refineries on the coast is that they really don't care about good P.R.] They do. They do. They do. They have to. Because we raise hell with them. (E – Jefferson)

In the last few years, the plants have gone beyond the committees.... Sterling Chemicals, for example – they, I know, have a neighborhood appreciation dinner where they bring people in what I call their impact zone, downwind. They bring them in, have them for dinner, and then take them on tours, give them explanations, show them their charts, open it up to questions. And it's a step in the right direction. Now, of course, you and I probably wouldn't know what kind of questions to ask. But at least you go out and see their plant in operation, and you see what actually goes on out there. It may, if not spur questions, at least open up some communication on it.... Those are the kinds of things I think that the plants are stressing to get back with the community. 'We want to be a good neighbor. We're a corporate neighbor, but we want to be a good neighbor.' For whatever reason. I don't know the motivation sometimes, but the end result is that there's more observation going on, and there's open communication and I think that's great. (G – Galveston)

I wouldn't say it's a perfect system, but the system works pretty well. Of course, one thing you have to remember is the city of Texas City is a big union town – the majority of those people that live there work there too. But that's not to say that those people don't call in and complain. We have a lot of eyes and ears out there constantly monitoring those facilities and they talk to the authorities when they think something is wrong. (G – Galveston)

I think those [CAPs] are excellent and I think every one of [the companies] ought to have one.... I just marvel at some of the things I've learned...the increased awareness just means so much to me. And I think if more people realized the measures that are being taken by the industry, they would appreciate the costs and the real problems the industry has to face. (B – Jefferson)

As might be expected, others were more skeptical:

[CAPs] provide an avenue, if you want to stick your neck out. And I think they expect no sticking of necks out. But there is the opportunity if you want to take advantage of it. I think it's like a one time only -- it's like a kamikaze event: once

48

you stick your neck out on it, you will never have another opportunity to do it. They will get another representative in your place.... I think it's a nice avenue for getting information from them. And, I think, in a sense, it's a good thing to have it. And if I were them, I wouldn't probably change a thing.... I think it's a win/win situation to some extent. It's more win for them than for us. (E – Jefferson)

The people who live there are really worried. And many of them feel that these Citizens' Advisory Panels are just propaganda, and in many respects I tend to agree. They didn't really buy into it...the residents don't believe the CAPs are doing anything. And that the people that go to those CAPs are being bought off by having their free lunch.... You feel pretty secure until something happens. And then the communication fails. (E – Nueces)

[CAPs] are corporate propaganda. They spend a great deal of money and a great deal of time spreading a blanket of ignorance over a community of people – uneducated people, generally. (E – Nueces)

[LEPCs] are of no use to people along refinery row.... It's not a workable plan. (E – Nueces)

We cannot get [the emergency radio station] in our neighborhood. We have to go get in the car and drive out of our neighborhood in order to hear it.... You cannot call anywhere and get any information.... And when you listen to that radio station, you get the Coastal Bend weather. You get how much refineries are doing for your neighborhood. (E – Nueces)

In many cases, respondents also reported that not very many people took advantage of these opportunities to communicate with industry officials until something bad happened, so it seems reasonable to assume that when they are not effective, both sides are probably responsible.

One example of increased cooperation between the industry and local residents that appears to be fairly widespread involves the relationship between company officials and environmental organizations. Both environmental activists and business representatives who were interviewed confirmed this general trend.

I think when it started out, the perception was that industry was just out to run roughshod and had a 'take no prisoners' attitude towards the environment and everything else. And, on the other hand, the environmentalists – the perception was that their number one agenda was to put everyone out of business. I think over the years they realized that industry is not as bad as they thought they were, and that the environmentalists weren't really trying to put everyone out of business – they just felt like they needed to pay attention to some things. I think they've hopefully overcome a lot of that. You've still got a few extremists on either side. Hopefully, common sense has prevailed, and we're moving forward. (G – Nueces)

49

The greater Houston area [is] unique, I think.... There aren't that many places where there have been tangible outcomes of consensus-building between traditional adversaries. In a lot of places, people are still fighting and throwing rocks at each other. In Houston...the organized environmental activists' community, and the organized business industry community, and the government folks... have been able to come together and agree to some things that would otherwise be very controversial.... (B – Harris)

The entire premise of the Galveston Bay Foundation, which is one of the more successful environmental organizations in the area, is to create a forum where industrial representatives and environmentalists can come together and discuss issues:

We try to walk a line. We're a balancing organization. We have a lot of industry involved in the Galveston Bay Foundation, and the whole philosophy of the Foundation has been to bring all the user groups together. And so, we have on our board commercial fishermen and operational fishermen, commercial navigation, recreational boating, industry, and environmental groups. All of them are represented on our board and among our membership. And so, we're constantly trying to walk the line, and making sure that the overall health of the Bay is maintained while everybody pretty much gets to continue the historical uses from the Bay system, but that things don't get too out of whack in one direction or another [Do you see yourself as a go-between?] Well, not exactly a go-between, because they're all sitting around the table with us.... I think that's what you have to do today. It's not longer viable – or probably never was viable, but it was perceived as viable – for people to set themselves up in camps and try to win battles. It's really important to try to find out where the common ground is and work together. (E – Harris)

Other environmentalists and business representatives that we talked to supported this approach, which seems like a very positive trend. It is perhaps indicative of the fact that the stereotypical "us vs. them" mentality among community members and industry in this region is gradually changing more generally. While there will always inherently be conflicting interests, some people appear to be experimenting with new ways of dealing with traditional conflicts.

## 4.5. Perceptions of Federal Government Involvement in Oil and Gas Issues

The involvement of the Minerals Management Service (MMS) and other federal agencies in the ongoing activities of the oil and gas industry is fairly significant, especially in the areas of leasing and regulation. It seemed important, then, to gather information from members of coastal communities about their perceptions of the role that the government plays in their area. Originally, this portion of the interview guide was designed to obtain data specifically on respondent's impressions of the MMS and their activities. However, only three of the people interviewed had ever even heard of the MMS, and even these three were not very familiar with what the MMS does in the region. After realizing that we would not be able to gather data specifically related to MMS, the question was broadened to include impressions about the proper role that the federal government more generally should play in local industry affairs.

Most respondents thought that the region had benefited significantly in the last 25 years from environmental regulations passed at the federal level, and that this was an appropriate role for Washington to play in the region. However, there were mixed opinions about how well the federal government truly understood local issues. One frequently expressed sentiment (especially from respondents in the business and governmental sectors) was that more environmental protection responsibility should be handed to state- and local-level governing entities:

> I don't think that they could do too much with oil and gas involvement. I think that has been more of the State's jurisdiction. I think that's probably better than any more involvement with the federal government.... I'm skeptical about the federal regulation getting into the oil and gas business. They just don't know what the local people who are in the field know about what the situation is. (G – Galveston)

> Of course, the main push is to give the power more to the states, to the local agencies to take care of. Of course, coming from a local agency, I'm in favor of that – to give a little more power to the states and the local programs. And my reasoning for that is: we're here – especially the local programs. We're here every day, day in and day out, we know the facilities, we know the problems better than anyone else. You know, EPA officials can come in and identify some problems, but they're in and out of town in a couple of days.... I really wish a lot of those powers would be given to the states – to give them more freedom and flexibility in what they're doing.... They know what the problems are. I mean, they communicate with this program on a daily basis, so they know. Not some administrator in Washington D.C. – they put out federal regulations that are supposed to cover the entire United States – and Maine and Texas are two different things, two different issues to deal with. (G – Galveston)

> I don't have any personal knowledge of MMS, but I have great confidence in our local system here – I think the federal government should back off. The locals in this community have more at stake, so let us deal with things that come up. (B – Galveston)

> I guess I'd have to come back and say, in the case of regulations, quite often it's the layers that become a problem. But it's: who do you want to deal with? I think in most cases, I'd rather deal with the State of Texas, because I think the state knows that we're different from Oklahoma or Arkansas, or Mississippi, in some regards. Some things we do very similar, and other things we have a whole different situation.... We would more than likely like to deal more, I think, with the state. I think they do understand that there is a difference between Beaumont and Odessa, or Lubbock and Houston. The feds have a hard time drawing distinctions. (G – Jefferson)

> We're perfectly capable of taking care of our own business. We don't mind taking the federal dollars to do the work, but I think we can accomplish a whole lot,

really, by being who we are and where we are, as opposed to having somebody in Washington or our regional office telling us what to do. (G – Nueces)

Let me say this: I don't care whether they're Democrats or Republicans, we've never had a coherent energy policy in this nation. Absent a coherent energy policy, I would just as soon the federal government get the hell out of it. They can set standards, but let the state agencies monitor them. Let the state agencies have oversight and just get away, because it's too cumbersome…. Give us a break. Give the people in the business a break. (B – Nueces)

I guess my biggest criticism is whether, it's the EPA or the TNRCC, or whatever, is that they run into the problem of drawing up regulations maybe on a cookie cutter approach that says, 'By golly, this is the way it is for Bangor, Maine, and that's the way it ought to be in Corpus Christi, Texas.' And they're worlds apart. Coming out of Washington or some of these other regulations, you've got a bunch of bureaucrats that have never really seen the issue at hand, but it looks good on paper. (G – Nueces)

Others thought that some federal regulatory requirements were either unfair, unjustified, or placed a financial burden on their community that was too high. One specific issue that came up several times in all of the refinery communities was that under the new produced air quality standards, it would be impossible for them to achieve attainment status in regard to acceptable ozone levels. This would limit possible development until their community was no longer classified as a non-attainment area.

One of the major issues on my mind is that they passed an Air Quality Act in 1990 or 1991…and they're trying to pass a new Air Quality Act that's going to reduce those numbers, and yet, our problems aren't created by our companies. Our problems aren't created by our community. They're created by things that are out of our control. So, if they're going to be fair, they need to enforce those rules on other areas…. They're going to pass rules that would adversely affect this community, and there's no proof that it's going to make for any better health…. [So focus on existing rules rather than passing new ones?] Absolutely, I mean, if they just get Houston to meet their rules of 1990 and 1991, it's going to help us, because it will make us an attainment area consistently…. (G – Jefferson)

We have problems and environmental concerns – the EPA. I fault them for the non-attainment classification in this area. A lot of it is because of mobile sources, and some of it's point sources, and some of it just naturally comes up through the marsh where all of this oil and gas is off the coast. (B – Jefferson)

There's things we can't control here. There are certain portions of environmental air quality problems that come from nature. There are certain portions of them that are coming in here from the Houston area by the prevailing winds that we have absolutely no control over. We get punished, or they've tried to punish us – because of the ozone level being exceeded on so many days and this type of thing.

Well, these proposed regulations that are pending right now, if those things go through, it's going to be very expensive to this area of the industry. Very expensive. They can kill you from expansions of the industry... nobody else could come in here. (G – Jefferson)

There was a time when we had to say, 'Hey, look fellows – look what we're doing to our environment.' And they did stop and they started spending their own money and improving things. And the regulations were instituted and they followed the regulations. But you've reached the point of diminishing returns.... I think we've done the same thing in environmental regulations that we do in so many things, human nature being what it is. And that is: if a little bit is good, a lot ought to be better.... And they keep tightening and tightening – without any consideration of whether the cost and the result are really justified. (G – Jefferson)

There's a real problem in that once a rule is made – I don't know if it's pride or the inability to say, 'I made a mistake.' But the federal government and the state government, to me, historically, have been totally inflexible in light of good solid evidence to admit they made a mistake or that their rule really needs to be changed. (G – Nueces)

My concern, and I've recognized it more since I have become active in local government, is that it seems when the federal government gets involved, you get a lot of mandates without funding. And then, who pays for it? The local people. I do not have any problem with the EPA – that's not my point. But my point is that as you get more into federal involvement, I think that what happens is, you wind up getting fined or taxed, or mandates. And you say, 'Now how do we do this and how do we pay for it?' And that's always my concern. (G – Galveston)

Other respondents (especially those from the environmental sector, of course) supported a strong federal regulatory role, and several noted that the industry had to be forced to take measures to protect the environment:

I want them staying in environmental issues. We, as counties or states, can't control big environmental issues. And I think the federal government should be in the environmental issues.... I think that the reason the oil and gas companies are responsive, and they have these things in place, is because they've been forced to. Were they not forced, they wouldn't. Everybody wants to rape the land, and take the benefits and go on unless there's some incentive there to do otherwise. (G – Aransas)

More regulations. And the reason I say that – people don't want any more regulations, but they don't do it on their own.... That's the real problem – how do we get people that are dealing in that industry to take responsibility for their actions? Do you regulate it? Do you give them economic incentive? Do you get their conscience?  Do you make their kids nag them at night?  What is the motivating factor for them to take care of the environment?  (E – Galveston)

Had we not had those laws in place, I don't think industry would have responded to do the things that have been done to make their atmosphere better.  (B – Galveston)

Improvements have been made, but begrudgingly.  I mean, the oil industry is not going to go out of its way to reduce its profits.  (E – Jefferson)

There is a great deal of discussion among environmental groups that are trying to work with industry, that it would be better, perhaps, to give them a monetary incentive?  In other words, 'If you do this, you get some tax credit' or something like that – rather than having a new law governing pollution.  (E – Nueces)

I would like to see clean air and water be a major issue in the current Legislature.  More legislation.  (E – Jefferson)

I think the federal government does have a role in leveling the playing field and making it so that everybody has to abide by the same basic socially, politically agreed upon goals.  And it's constantly a balancing act about who, socially and politically, they're going to listen to.  (E – Harris)

There's no question that we needed federal standards...  The truth is, if you've got a national market, you've got companies literally operating on both sides of the same river in different states, and one of them can't afford to put in pollution control devices if their competition isn't.  So, you had to have national standards, and that was a good thing.  (B – Nueces)

The federal government has a big role in all of this, but that's the kind of regulation and the kind of response that the government should have.  I'm not saying that they should take responsibility away from the industry.  The federal government has a role in both regulating and enforcing.  (E – Nueces)

I think they need to make sure that the regulations that we have are being enforced.  We've got a hell of a lot down on paper.  And there's actually not anybody to enforce a lot of it, especially once you get offshore.  The Coast Guard...can't do it.  The EPA is way understaffed as far as field people are concerned.  And the same thing is true of the State agencies.  Everybody's sitting in offices!  (E – Jefferson)

Two people mentioned that they would like to see the federal government work on getting international environmental regulations in place and enforced.  The coastal community is vulnerable to environmental threats from other countries that do not require the same safeguards as does the U.S.:

I guess my primary interest would be in the ships or barges – transporting, and their construction go to the double-wall construction that will hopefully provide a little more protection [from spills]. (G – Nueces)

I think for us, probably the major thing is enforcing some of the international laws so that these ships can't throw their trash and everything offshore. Figuring out how to enforce that, and what kinds of penalties to have. That would be a tremendous help to us. And then, I guess, just strengthening the reaction to any kind of spill – respond to it quickly and do everything possible to see that it doesn't happen, whether it's having those double liners on the ships or whatever. Those kinds of regulations and things I guess could help us in the long run. (B – Nueces)

Other respondents supplied a variety of ideas about the roles they would like to see the federal government play in their communities:

If they could come in here and have some impact on erosion, which nobody has been able to solve, I think anybody would welcome that. (G – Aransas)

Grant programs – funding programs for communities.... We need funding in a lot of cases, and the federal government takes a lot from us with oil and gas. (B – Aransas)

They could help us diversify by a lot of grants.... This may be farfetched, and it may be off-base, but because of the down-time, because of the reliance in the past, because of some of the regulations that have come out about the environment – that's causing the automation...there have been job displacements because of that. They could help us retrain people. They could help develop this area in diversity, in trying to get other jobs. (B – Jefferson)

Education. First of all, education, education, education – at all levels. [About what?] Well, about water, soil, and air – those three. There's different ways of looking at each of those three things. And for Galveston, we have such a concentration along the Gulf Coast of people [and] of our state product, and I just think that we need to become more aware of how integrated everybody is becoming as the years go on. It's becoming a smaller and smaller world, and I just think that there needs to be more of an integration of people understanding how things affect them.... (G – Galveston)

I think there's more health hazards that need to be publicized by the federal government. Periodically – once every two years – there is a list compiled of related deaths, such as 'if you live in this area, you're going to have more toxic, cancer-related deaths, and they come from these kinds of exposures.' And there are some people more susceptible to that kind of stuff, and I think people need to know if they live within a three-mile radius of a plant that has those kinds of emissions, and are prone to getting that, they stand a higher risk of that. If the

55

federal government is going to allow a company to be in business to do that kind of stuff, there needs to be a disclosure in that community of those kinds of [risks]. (G – Galveston)

I think the feds are going to have to become involved in the environmental clean up and the recovery of our lands and waters that were damaged as a result of activities in the 50s, 60s, and 70s.  And I say that because everywhere we turn, our real terrors are these time bombs we find.... The next big challenge is going to be cleaning up what was done prior to regulation, because some of the contamination we're talking about is not going to disappear.  (G – Nueces)

Although some of the comments above reflect the current national trend toward support for less governmental influence at the federal level, no one denied that their community was in much better shape environmentally than before the wave of federal environmental legislation passed in the 1970s and 80s.  There were more conflicting opinions over how many more regulations were needed, and who should pay for and enforce those that are already on the books.

## 5. Summary and Conclusions

The data in this study confirm the fact that the Texas coastal region remains highly dependent on the oil and gas industry.  The industry provides more employment opportunities and more tax revenue to the communities in this area than does any other source.  It is also fair to say that the whole social infrastructure of many coastal communities was built around the needs of the industry.  This dependency continues, in spite of the industry's 1980s bust cycle and in spite of some communities' continuing efforts to diversify economically.  Indeed, the whole idea of identifying "stakeholder groups" in this area seems far too limiting – it is difficult to find any group or sector in these communities that does not have some "stake" in industry activities.

Given this level of dependency, it would be easy to oversimplify the social and economic issues salient to the people in coastal communities.  In actuality, the relationships between the oil and gas industry and the communities that host its various activities is a complex one, perhaps best viewed as a series of balances between competing interests, needs, values, and goals.  An understanding of the social and economic benefits provided to the population in this region by the strong local presence of the industry must be accompanied by an understanding of the vulnerabilities that these same benefits generate.

For example, the employment opportunities provided by the industry in the region are essential to the ongoing survival of many communities.  On the other hand, this dependency (not only on industry jobs, but also on those in support businesses) creates a constant strain of uncertainty on individuals as well as on various non-industry entities, such as local governments and service providers.  The primary lesson that came from the 1980s bust was, after all, that the oil and gas industry is very volatile and "what's here today may not be here tomorrow."  Even tax revenues received from oil and gas companies can not necessarily be counted on, as the current situation in Jefferson County illustrates.  How, then, are community and individual level planning issues to be approached?

One solution to this dilemma has been to try to provide a local context in which the industry can thrive, in order to encourage continuing industry expansion and growth. Cities have offered generous tax abatements, "in lieu of" tax agreements, and even exemptions from environmental regulations in the name of keeping industry activities in their local area. Yet, at the same time cities are trying to encourage local industry growth, the needs of the industry have necessitated corporate downsizing in recent years. For example, one way the industry pulled out of its slump in the 1980s was to invest in automation, which reduces the number of employees, required to maintain its operations.

Another response has been to try to encourage other industries (e.g., high-tech companies in Houston) or government projects (e.g., prison construction in Jefferson County) to come to the community in order to diversify local economies. Diversification has been more successful in some areas than others, but nowhere have the returns on these efforts equaled the region's historical and continuing investment in the oil and gas industry. Some areas have gone so far as to abandon nearly all direct ties to the industry by focusing on tourism almost exclusively, but even these communities remain tied to oil and gas because they rely on the industry salaries that enable people to take advantage of their recreational and real estate opportunities.

All of these approaches make logical sense from a local planning standpoint, but, to date, none has altered the basic fact that these communities probably can not survive (or at least thrive) without the continued presence and success of oil and gas. The bottom line is, industry interests do not always coincide with the interests of their host communities. Specific companies do make considerable contributions in the form of donations of money or volunteer support for numerous community projects and organizations, but it is no surprise that, ultimately, their primary commitment is internal – to their own profit margins.

Another area of competing interests involves local concerns about environmental protection, on the one hand, and the environmental risks inherently associated with both upstream and downstream industry activities on the other. Even the relationship between environmental activists and industry officials, however, is not as simple as it might first appear. The stereotypical notion of "no-growth environmentalists" vs. "uncaring industry" is far too black-and-white to accurately describe the relationship between these two groups in Texas coastal communities. In fact, after years of interaction, the trend in many communities is toward increased dialogue, more effective communication, and even the development of consensus-building activities involving these two interest groups.

The biggest concern in all of the communities represented in this study was environmental degradation linked to industry activities. Areas heavily invested in tourism were especially worried about oil spills and beach tar and trash, while other areas were most concerned with the air and water pollution produced by refining and petrochemical complexes. Drilling and exploration activities also inevitably compromise the purity of wetlands and bay and Gulf waters. The industry has responded to the general environmental consciousness that has increased over the past 25 or 30 years in the region (and the country) by spending millions of dollars to improve air and water quality in its host communities. Many business and government leaders praise these efforts, even as environmental groups call for more. On the other hand, most of the environmentalists we interviewed readily conceded the improvements that had taken place, and most business representatives expressed the need for further clean-up efforts. Common beliefs about the "proper use of the environment" were widespread – the issue for both groups was how to achieve this goal while, at the same time, making it possible for the oil and gas industry to continue its local operations.

Given all of these differing interests, it is not surprising that the relationship between coastal communities and the industry varies widely across the region – from complacent or ambivalent in regions where industry activities are less visible, to distrustful and contentious in locations immediately adjacent to refinery complexes. One key factor here is that when the population in an area feels that they are contributing (or losing) more to the industry than they are getting back (e.g., living with the pollution produced by refineries, but not getting jobs in the plants), they are more likely to respond negatively to industry presence. This often accounts for differences in relations with the industry found within the same city. For those who live in more highly affected areas, the industry is seen as more of a liability, while for those who live further away and are not consciously affected negatively on a daily basis, industry is viewed as an asset to the community. The same difference applies to groups who feel more or less empowered to influence industry activities – feelings of helplessness and exposure to risk lead to a more negative reaction to industry presence.

This later situation is what has led to the ongoing environmental justice movements in Corpus Christi and Jefferson County. Some groups are accusing the industry and local governments of actively discriminating against poor and minority residents living in refinery neighborhoods. Respondents from the business and government sectors see this accusation as unjustified because there has been no intentional discrimination. Both groups may be correct in their assessments of the situation, but the problem remains unresolved, and the differences of opinion on the matter have to do with issues of power and efficacy in relation to the industry. This basic perspective also explains why the relationship between business and government officials tends to be more felicitous than that between some citizen groups and either industry or government entities. It should also be noted that simply providing opportunities for increased communication between industry officials and community members (such as CAPs) is not a solution in and of itself. These programs are largely unsuccessful if public trust and feelings of efficacy are low.

Respondents' opinions about the proper role for the federal government to play in the region varied a great deal as well. Most environmentalists supported federal-level environmental regulation, while individuals from the business and government sectors were more sensitive to the external controls such regulations imposed. They generally favored more local control, reasoning that "the bureaucrats in Washington" did not have a clear understanding of local issues. However, both sides agreed that probably the only reason the state of the region's environment had improved in the last two decades was that federal legislation had required it. Government and business leaders were generally more aware of the costs incurred (by local governments and the industry) in the process of achieving these improvements, while environmentalists were more likely to define the issue as a moral or ethical one. Once again, respondents' positions in the structural arena of the community influenced their perspectives.

It appears that there is a continuing role for the federal government to play in this region, especially in the area of environmental policy. However, efforts in this area should be approached with sensitivity to the complexity of the issues salient to different groups within these communities. It is hoped that this report has contributed to a better understanding of these issues, and that further work will be done to follow up the findings presented here. The recent renewal of industry activity in the Texas coastal region presents a good opportunity to focus on establishing improved relations and communication between various sections of the communities in this area, and the feeling of cautious optimism expressed by many informants provides a good context for such endeavors.

## COMPLETED DISCUSSIONS WITH KEY INFORMANTS

### Government

David Bowers, Galveston City Council
Larry Edrozo, Texas City City Council
Bob Allen, Port Arthur City Council
Gracie Guzman Saenz, Houston City Council
Judge Carl Griffith, Jefferson County Judge
Ed Stuart, Galveston County Commissioner
Steve Raddack, Harris County Commissioner
Ray Riley, City Manager, Beaumont
Judge Agnes Hardin, Aransas County Judge
Pete Gildon, Rockport City Manager
Joe McComb, Nueces County Commissioner
Chris Lawrence, assist. to Nueces County Judge
Tom Brooks, Port Aransas City Manager
Wayne Jordan, Aransas County Navigation District
Oscar Pina, Aransas County Commissioner
Buddy Stanley, TNRCC, Corpus Christi

### Business

John Tindel, Galveston Chamber of Commerce
Jimmy Hayley, Texas City Chamber of Commerce
Verna Rutherford, Pt. Arthur Chamber of Commerce
Buzz Elton, Hotel/Motel Assoc., Galveston
Mike Mulvihill, Home Owners Assoc., Galveston
David Bernsen, SE Texas Inc., Beaumont
Diane Probst, Rockport-Fulton Chamber of Commerce
Becky Corder, local realtor in Port Aransas (also on school board)
Jim Kachtick, Oxychem in Houston
Charlie Herbeck, Attorney in Texas City
Kent Fuller, Greater Houston Partnership
Carol Ann Anderson, Port Aransas Chamber of Commerce
Gary Bushell, Greater Corpus Christi Business Alliance
Dick Bowers, Port Commission and businessman, Corpus Christi

### Environmental

Judy and Saul Aronow, Golden Triangle Sierra Club (Beaumont)
Linda Shead, Galveston Bay Foundation

Marge Hanselman, Houston Sierra Club (Conservation Chair)
Richard Harrell, Clean Air and Water, Inc., Beaumont
Bill Green, People Against a Contaminated Environment, Corpus Christi
Tony Amos, U.T. Marine Science Institute (Port Aransas)
Jackie Cole, env. activist in Galveston
Ronnie Schultz, Galveston Co. Pollution Control
Pat Suter, Sierra Club, Corpus Christi
Zelma Champion, env. activist in Corpus Christi


(Totals by county and category):

Aransas County - total: 5
    gov. – 4
    bus. – 1
    env. – 0

Galveston County - total: 10
    gov. – 3
    bus. – 5
    env. – 2

Harris County - total: 6
    gov. – 2
    bus. – 2
    env. – 2

Jefferson County - total: 7
    gov. – 3
    bus. – 2
    env. – 2

Nueces County- total: 12
    gov. – 4
    bus. – 4
    env. – 4

OVERALL TOTAL: 40
    government- 16
    business – 14
    environmental - 10

(+ telephone interviews with:
    2 state legislative staff members
    6 local media reps.)

## APPENDIX B

## POTENTIAL DISCUSSION TOPICS

### Public Awareness/Concerns

Do you think people in this (city, town, community) have concerns about any potentially negative effects of oil and gas development activity?

> If so, what are these concerns?
> How uniform are these concerns within the (city, town, community)?

How would your community be affected if there were a downturn in oil and gas activity in the Gulf of Mexico?

Is your community's socioeconomic make-up significantly different today than, say, 20 (10?) years ago?

> If so, how have these changes in the structure of the community changed the outlook towards offshore oil development?

What is the local public's general attitude toward/perception of off- and onshore oil activities?

What are the major concerns and what are perceived as major benefits?

What are the risks (social costs) that impacted local residents associate with oil and gas related activities in the community?

What potential impacts are local residents most concerned about?
> e.g. - environmental, economic, way of life, public services, local infrastructure?

In general, do you think that local residents in this area see the recent increase in oil and gas activity as an "opportunity for" or a "threat to" the stability of the community? (Why?)

### Communication with/Feedback from Local Community

How do local parties (both for and against development) first find out about a proposed oil-related project or activity?

At what stage of planning do they usually find out?

How willing are the oil industry officials in your area to share information about planned development projects with the community?

Do the oil companies in your area provide any sort of public forum opportunity or clear feedback mechanisms to get input from the community on planned developments? (Examples?)

> If so, do many people take advantage of these opportunities?

> If so, do you think this feedback affects the decisions of the companies concerning how to proceed with development?

Do you think that people in this community feel that they have any power over decisions about local oil and gas development?

How well do you think the state and local officials in your area know their rights concerning the various statutes and laws that govern oil and gas development?

## Environmental Concerns

The environmental movement is much stronger across the country today than it was in the 1970s - has this change affected your community's outlook toward offshore oil development?

Are the environmental concerns that affect the people in this community being adequately addressed?

Have any of the coastal communities that rely on fishing (commercial or recreational) noticed any effects (positive or negative) of the recent increases in offshore oil activities?

Have any of the local communities that depend on tourism revenues experienced a negative impact on their tourism trade due to litter and debris on their beaches?

If yes, was the increased litter and debris attributable to offshore oil and gas development activities?

Have any specific steps been taken to deal with this problem?

## Planning

How dependent do you think this community is on the oil and gas industry?

Do you think this local dependence is less or greater than it was ten years ago? (Why?)

How do oil development activities affect this community's social, educational and economic conditions?

To what extent do potential impacts depend on: a) the community's involvement in resource extraction, and b) whether the community is involved primarily in related industries such as refining, wholesaling, metal fabrication, shipping, etc.?

Do you think that the potential impacts are mostly positive, mostly negative, or a mixture? (Examples?)

If potentially negative impacts have been identified, what are some of the ways these impacts can be mitigated? (Or: How can a coastal community protect itself from the inherent volatility associated with a resource extraction industry?)

What are local officials in your area doing to protect the (city, community) from potentially harmful social and economic effects of increased oil and gas development?

Are local officials aware of the vast amounts of literature and research that are available to assist them in planning for the potential impacts of oil and gas activity?

> If yes, what types of materials do they use and what do they use them for?
> If no, are there specific types of material that would assist in them in local planning?

Are programs in place to, for instance, channel oil facilities into priority employment and investment areas?

> If yes, are these programs being developed together with mechanisms for mediating possible conflicts between environmental protection and economic development policies?

If necessary, who will finance the additional cost of public services that would be necessary to maintain existing service levels?

Have the effects of offshore activities in the following areas been considered in local planning?
- fishing (commercial, subsistence, and recreational)
- local tourism and recreation
- national security (military)- e.g. harbor facilities, navigation and overflight losses
- marine transportation - e.g. changing shipping routes, added risk of collision with offshore platforms
- other industries in the area that compete for scarce resources
- increased water supply demands
- financing for general capital improvements

Has your local community already come to grips with the possibility that there may never again be an increase in resource extraction-based employment?

When oil and gas activities pick up in your area, are locals the first to be recruited for on- and offshore jobs?

To what extent, if any, are there regional plans in place to insure that the local community and region benefit from the increased amount of oil and gas activity?

What are the potential effects of increased oil and gas related activities on:
- local employment
- non-related local industries
- local medical and educational facilities
- local tax bases
- local water supplies
- community and local governments
- other local organizations
- local crime rates

Who are the local powers and decisionmakers in this community?

How well do you think they represent the views of the community?

How do they perceive industrial development vs. other forms of development, such as tourism, retirement facilities, etc.?

Do you think your community has adequately addressed the potential local costs of increased oil and gas activity?

    If yes, how?
    If no, why not? And how might this type of consideration be encouraged in the future?

## The Department of the Interior Mission

As the Nation's principal conservation agency, the Department of the Interior has responsibility for most of our nationally owned public lands and natural resources. This includes fostering sound use of our land and water resources; protecting our fish, wildlife, and biological diversity; preserving the environmental and cultural values of our national parks and historical places; and providing for the enjoyment of life through outdoor recreation. The Department assesses our energy and mineral resources and works to ensure that their development is in the best interests of all our people by encouraging stewardship and citizen participation in their care. The Department also has a major responsibility for American Indian reservation communities and for people who live in island territories under U.S. administration.

## The Minerals Management Service Mission

As a bureau of the Department of the Interior, the Minerals Management Service's (MMS) primary responsibilities are to manage the mineral resources located on the Nation's Outer Continental Shelf (OCS), collect revenue from the Federal OCS and onshore Federal and Indian lands, and distribute those revenues.

Moreover, in working to meet its responsibilities, the **Offshore Minerals Management Program** administers the OCS competitive leasing program and oversees the safe and environmentally sound exploration and production of our Nation's offshore natural gas, oil and other mineral resources. The MMS **Minerals Revenue Management** meets its responsibilities by ensuring the efficient, timely and accurate collection and disbursement of revenue from mineral leasing and production due to Indian tribes and allottees, States and the U.S. Treasury.

The MMS strives to fulfill its responsibilities through the general guiding principles of: (1) being responsive to the public's concerns and interests by maintaining a dialogue with all potentially affected parties and (2) carrying out its programs with an emphasis on working to enhance the quality of life for all Americans by lending MMS assistance and expertise to economic development and environmental protection.

www.ingramcontent.com/pod-product-compliance
Lightning Source LLC
Chambersburg PA
CBHW052010280526
45793CB00005B/918

* 9 7 8 1 5 0 5 5 0 1 4 3 8 *